SEEDS OF TRUST

Reflecting on the Bible in Silence and Song

Also available from the Taizé Community, published by
GIA Publications, Inc.:

God Is Love Alone (G-6259)

Prayer for Each Day (G-4918)

The Sources of Taizé (G-5363)

G-6719

SEEDS OF TRUST

Reflecting on the Bible in Silence and Song

TAIZÉ

GIA Publications, Inc.
Chicago

ISBN: 1-57999-538-1
(USA, Canada, and USA dependencies)

G-6719

Scripture quotations are from the New Revised Standard Version of the Bible, copyright © 1989 by the Division of Christian Education of the National Council of Churches in Christ in the USA. Used by permission. All rights reserved.

All songs © Ateliers et Presses de Taizé
Music: J. S. Bach (page 28), Jacques Berthier (pages 12, 14, 20, 22, 24, 26, 30, 36, 38, 40, 42, 46, 50, 52, 56, 58, 60, 62, 64, 66, 72, 74, 78, 80, 86, 88, 92, 94, 96, 106, 110, 112, 114, 120, 128, 130, 132, 136, 138, 142), Joseph Gelineau (pages 16, 124), Orthodox tradition (pages 101, 118, 134), Taizé (18, 34, 44, 48, 68, 70, 82, 84, 90, 104, 108, 116, 126, 140).

GIA Publications, Inc.
7404 S. Mason Ave., Chicago, IL 60638
www.giamusic.com

Contents

REDISCOVERING HOPE

GOING FORWARD WITH DISCERNMENT

LEARNING TO LOVE

Introduction

Meditating on the Bible means becoming part of a story of love and of trust.[1] A story of love, because it reveals both God's infinite love[2] and his burning desire that each person,[3] discovering that they are loved, may wish one day to love God with all their heart in return.[4] A story of trust, because scripture discloses a God who, even when rejected and abandoned, still keeps believing in human beings,[5] loving them to the end[6], and doing all in his power to awaken their trust.[7] Yes, a story of love and trust, because throughout the Bible it is as though God invited each of us personally to trust in his love and to place our confidence in him, so as to enter into a communion that will have no end.

In order to put down deep roots in the human heart and be brought to fruition there over time, however, this trust needs first of all to overcome a host of fears, worries, and difficulties, and then constantly to be nourished, protected, and renewed. This book wishes to play a small part in helping such trust to grow. It offers sixty short Bible meditations written by brothers of the Taizé Community.[8] These meditations have been divided into six chapters describing an inner journey: *discovering a love* greater than anything we could have imagined; going *to the wellsprings of forgiveness*, where God understands everything and liberates us; being led by God *toward an inner healing*, so indispensable to keep going forward; *rediscovering hope* rooted in love; *going forward with discernment* in freedom and confidence; and *learning to love* more and more intensely.

In addition to the relevant Bible text, each of the short meditations is followed by questions, a song from Taizé, and a prayer written by the founder of the Taizé Community, Brother Roger. These last two elements serve as a reminder that the purpose of reflecting on the Bible, even if it is followed by a time of discussion, is not to lead us to empty spiritual chatter, but rather to support the development of an interpersonal relationship with someone who loves us.

In practical terms, the different elements in this book can be made use of in different ways. They can be used first of all for personal reflection. If studies or work do not leave much time for long periods of silence, one can take half an hour or an hour from time to time to enter a church, to kneel before an icon in one's room, or to find solitude in nature. There, in silence, one can meditate on a passage from scripture that speaks to the heart, praying to God with one of the prayers provided here or even singing to oneself.

This book can also be used for a time of sharing with others. For example, a few friends from the same church or town can meet to read the Bible text together aloud; then they can spend thirty minutes or an hour in silence before ending with a time of sharing and a moment of prayer together. If it is difficult to meet together at the same time, a day can be set in advance when each person will read and reflect on the text at whatever time they wish. Then, in the evening, all can meet at church or in the home of one of the participants for a short discussion and a prayer. Others may decide to read and reread the same text in the course of an entire month and then, when they have thoroughly assimilated it, to come together for a time of sharing. Finally, whether in a church or student group or an informal group of friends, it is possible to sing the songs;[9] in this way, reflection on the Bible will go hand in hand with an attempt to contemplate the beauty of God through music.

Notes

[1] See Psalm 13:5

[2] See, for example, 1 John 4:8,16; 1 John 1:5; John 15:9–12; Romans 5:6–8; Romans 8:31–38; Ephesians 2:4–10; Psalms 103; Jeremiah 31:3; Hosea 2:18–23; and Zephaniah 3:17.

[3] See 1 Timothy 2:4

[4] See Matthew 22:37

[5] See John 21:15–17 and Luke 23:34

[6] See Nehemiah 9:16–19 and John 13:1

[7] See Matthew 9:2, 22; Matthew 17:7; Luke 12:7–32; and John 6:20

[8] They were published previously in the *Letter from Taizé*.

[9] Instrumental accompaniments and solo verses can be found in the publications listed at *www.taize.fr*.

DISCOVERING A LOVE

The Free Gift of God's Love

God, who is rich in mercy, out of the great love with which he loved us even when we were dead through our trespasses, made us alive together with Christ—by grace you have been saved—and raised us up with him and seated us with him in the heavenly places in Christ Jesus, so that in the ages to come he might show the immeasurable riches of his grace in kindness toward us in Christ Jesus. For by grace you have been saved through faith, and this is not your own doing; it is the gift of God—not the result of works, so that no one may boast. For we are what he has made us, created in Christ Jesus for good works, which God prepared beforehand to be our way of life.

– Ephesians 2:4–10

Toi, tu nous aimes / *Lord God, you love us*

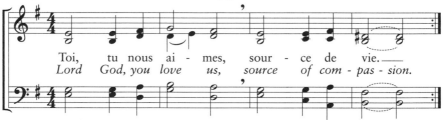

The author of the Letter to the Ephesians announces and celebrates the free gift of God's love. In spite of the fact that "we were dead through our trespasses…, by grace [we] have been saved" (Ephesians 2:5). For Saint Paul, grace is the foundation of the Christian life. Salvation is a gift from God. We do not earn salvation like a salary after doing our work well. We are saved because God is rich in mercy and tenderness and because "all God can do is give his love" (Isaac of Nineveh, seventh century).

In the Old Testament, one of the prophets understood well that God loves his people unconditionally—the prophet Isaiah. In a passage read each year during the Easter Vigil, Isaiah says to his people, "Everyone who thirsts, come to the waters; and you that have no money, come, buy and eat! Come, buy wine and milk without money and without price" (Isaiah 55:1–11).

In the New Testament, this love has become a person: Jesus, the Christ. Jesus never spoke the word grace. But by his actions and his words, by his forgiveness and by giving his life freely, he showed us the depths of his love. And Jesus invites us to live in the same way he did. The free gift of God's love does not turn us into people who are passive. This love "make[s] us alive" with Christ (Ephesians 2:5) and makes us able to dare to give our life for others. Then a miracle can take place in our existence: we begin to love as God loved us. Still more: God begins to love in us. "We are what he has made us, created in Christ Jesus for good works, which God prepared beforehand to be our way of life" (Ephesians 2:10).

- When have I had an experience of unconditional love in my life?
- How did this experience affect or even change my life? What other Bible texts, words, or actions of Jesus help me to understand the words of the Letter to the Ephesians, "we are saved by grace," by the free gift of God's love?

Breath of God's loving, Holy Spirit, if we place our trust in you, it is because you lead us to discover this surprising reality: God creates neither fear nor anguish in us; all God can do is love.

God Is Tenderness

Bless the Lord, O my soul,
and all that is within me, bless his holy name.
Bless the Lord, O my soul
and do not forget all his benefits —
who forgives all your iniquity,
who heals all your diseases,
who redeems your life from the Pit,
who crowns you with steadfast love and mercy,
who satisfies you with good as long as you live
so that your youth is renewed like the eagle's.
The Lord works vindication
and justice for all who are oppressed.
He made known his ways to Moses,
his acts to the people of Israel
The Lord is merciful and gracious,
slow to anger and abounding in steadfast love.
He will not always accuse,
nor will he keep his anger forever.
He does not deal with us according to our sins,
nor repay us according to our iniquities.
For as the heavens are high above the earth,
so great is his steadfast love toward those who fear him;
as far as the east is from the west,
so far he removes our transgressions from us.
As a father has compassion for his children,
so the Lord has compassion for those who fear him...
Bless the Lord, all his works.

— Psalm 103:1–13, 22

Bless the Lord

Bless the Lord, my soul, and bless God's ho-ly name. —

Bless the Lord, my soul, who leads me in-to life.

This psalm is a powerful celebration of God's love. Different images evoke God's inexhaustible efficacy and sensitivity. This confession, born of a personal experience, develops in two directions that come to a climax in the invitations that open and close the prayer: "Bless the Lord, O my soul!" "Bless the Lord, all his works!"

Thankfulness for God's intervention leads to knowledge of God's will and ways of acting, both in the lives of individuals and in the history of the nation. It leads believers to desire that love more and more, so that it can give life to their entire being.

In addition, the assurance of God's unlimited kindness enables believers to take off all their masks and recognize that they are poor and vulnerable, but at the same time free and called to an intimate collaboration with God. They can then look at others as God does: rooted in God's own life, they are unable to nurture resentment or return evil for evil. Their relationships with others will change. Worshippers discover a responsibility for drawing all creation along with them and reawakening in each person the desire to welcome God's love in order to praise him always.

- How did Jesus live out God's love celebrated in this psalm?
- What in me does not yet participate in this blessing?
- How, in our day, can we invite a world that does not know God to bless God?

Jesus, our hope, even were we weak and destitute, our deepest desire would be to understand that you love us. You shed light on the road leading to heartfelt compassion.

All God Can Do Is Love

Therefore, I will now allure her, and bring her into the wilderness, and speak tenderly to her. From there I will give her her vineyards, and make the Valley of Achor a door of hope. There she shall respond as in the days of her youth, as at the time when she came out of the land of Egypt.

— Hosea 2:14–15

Dieu ne peut que donner son amour /
God can only give faithful love

"All God can do is love." Few believers have understood this as well as the prophet Hosea, even though he lived eight centuries before Christ. Hosea discovered this truth and expressed it in his life as a prophet. Although several prophets made use of symbols, the symbol Hosea found was quite dramatic and intense. To express God's relationship with the people, Hosea was asked to take a prostitute for his wife and to love her. He had to put up with her unfaithfulness. What was the prophet thinking about? Political alliances with other nations? Perhaps even more than that, the fact that Israel continually turned to other gods to ensure the fertility of the land, of their flocks, and of their families.

There is also anger in Hosea. It explodes in chapter 2. God can take it no more. He has done all he can for this nation, and yet they always turn to others. The reasons for this anger are mentioned three times, in the form of a lawsuit. And each time the appropriate punishment is expressed by the formula: "that is why..." For the third and final summing up of Israel's unfaithfulness, the reader expects that the punishment mentioned will be even greater. And instead we find these words: "Therefore, I will now allure her, and bring her into the wilderness, and speak tenderly to her... She shall respond as in the days of her youth." And in the following chapter, we see Hosea take back his unfaithful wife and love her as she is.

Jesus, whom the Gospels refer to as the "Bridegroom," liked to quote Hosea. During a meal with sinners, a celebration where there was no fasting because the Bridegroom was present, Jesus justified his behavior by recalling God's words in Hosea: "I desire steadfast love and not sacrifice" (6:6). He did not come to accuse his people. In him there is "more than a prophet"—someone who can give a brand-new love to all.

- What does the symbolism of marriage, which Hosea is the first to use, tell us about God?
- Why does Hosea announce a promise when we would expect to find a punishment? What has he understood about God?

Risen Christ, when we have the simple desire to welcome your love, little by little a flame is kindled in the depths of our being. Fuelled by the Holy Spirit, it may be quite faint. But it keeps on burning. And when we realize that you love us, the trust of faith becomes our own song.

A Love Offered to All

*One of the dinner guests, on hearing this, said to him,
"Blessed is anyone who will eat bread in the kingdom of
God!" Then Jesus said to him, "Someone gave a great
dinner and invited many. At the time for the dinner he
sent his slave to say to those who had been invited,
'Come; for everything is ready now.' But they all alike
began to make excuses. The first said to him, 'I have
bought a piece of land, and I must go out and see it;
please accept my regrets.' Another said, 'I have bought
five yoke of oxen, and I am going to try them out; please
accept my regrets.' Another said, 'I have just been
married, and therefore I cannot come.' So the slave
returned and reported this to his master. Then the owner
of the house became angry and said to his slave, 'Go out
at once into the streets and lanes of the town and bring
in the poor, the crippled, the blind, and the lame.' And
the slave said, 'Sir, what you ordered has been done, and
there is still room.' Then the master said to the slave, 'Go
out into the roads and lanes, and compel people to come
in, so that my house may be filled.'"*

– Luke 14:15–23

The kingdom of God

The king - dom of God is jus - tice and peace and
joy in the Ho - ly Spir - it. Come, Lord, and
o - pen in us the gates of your king - dom. The

How many times was Jesus confronted with the questions: What is God's kingdom like? How can we enter it? People's expectations were so different: will this kingdom come with power, or is it always put off till later, like a longed-for promise?

"One of the dinner guests said to Jesus...." Here again we are at a meal, as so often in Saint Luke's Gospel. Jesus is the one who eats with us. How can people be closer than to be seated at the same table? And so Jesus will use this image to explain how God waits for us and invites us.

In the Gospel according to Saint Matthew, the meal is a wedding banquet for the son of a king. How is it possible that the invited guests could have forgotten the date? They are invited twice. How can they put their own business first, even if it is important, when this meal represents the most essential event for the future of the kingdom? It is the poor, the lame, and the blind who are able to accept the invitation and enter into God's joy, because they cannot take care of their own business: they are dependent on others for everything. Jesus is close to death, and so perhaps feels even closer to all who are abandoned and forgotten. He understands that, through his resurrection, all humanity will be able to welcome God's love.

In the face of incomprehensible forgetfulness, and even at times refusal, Jesus reveals the image of the Father's generosity. All people are invited to be part of this communion, and it is through this incredible gift that the kingdom is revealed.

- How can we recognize those times when God's kingdom becomes manifest, when communion becomes possible with Christ and with others?
- The festive meal is offered without conditions. How can we remain open and enter day after day into the joy that is offered to us?

Christ Jesus, even if your resurrection only kindled a tiny flame within us, it would enable us to live in communion with you. And by your Gospel we realize that you came to earth not just for part of humankind but for all human beings, even if they are unaware of your presence within them.

"I Will Never Forsake You"

Jesus said to his disciples, "If you love me, you will keep my commandments. And I will ask the Father, and he will give you another Advocate, to be with you forever. This is the Spirit of truth, whom the world cannot receive, because it neither sees him nor knows him. You know him, because he abides with you, and he will be in you. "I will not leave you orphaned; I am coming to you. In a little while the world will no longer see me, but you will see me; because I live, you also will live. On that day you will know that I am in my Father, and you in me, and I in you."

– John 14:15–20

Tui amoris ignem / *Holy Spirit, come to us*

Ve - ni Sanc - te Spi - ri - tus, tu - i a - mo - ris
Ho - ly Spir - it, come to us, kin - dle in us the

i - gnem ac - cen - de. Ve - ni Sanc - te
fire of your love. Ho - ly Spir - it,

Spi - ri - tus, ve - ni Sanc - te Spi - ri - tus.
come to us, Ho - ly Spir - it, come to us.

Jesus knows the human heart. He knew that his death on the cross would be a scandal for his disciples. That is why, before giving his life, he asked his Father to give them "another Advocate," in other words, a helper, a support. The first meaning of this word comes from the law courts; it refers to the attorney who stands beside the person accused of a crime.

How is the Holy Spirit a defender, a support, a comforter? If Jesus says he will ask the Father for "*another* Advocate," that is because he sees himself as the first support. To understand how the Holy Spirit is at work in our lives, we must therefore look first to see how Jesus supported and comforted his companions. The Holy Spirit is for us what Jesus was for his disciples and for those who met him.

For the evangelist John, the Holy Spirit is also the Spirit of truth. Since God is beyond our human understanding, we need help to see "the whole truth." The Holy Spirit will help us to understand first the truth about God, who loves each of us without exception, and then the truth about Jesus, the Son of God, who makes God's love accessible to us by giving his life on a cross. Then the cross no longer appears as a failure or an absurdity (see 1 Corinthians 1:18–25), but the revelation of the mystery of God's love.

The Spirit of truth will also teach us the truth about ourselves. Sometimes, the voices that accuse us are not voices from the outside, but those by which we accuse ourselves. We see our weak points, and this leads to doubt and discouragement. The Holy Spirit comes to help us understand that even if our hearts condemn us, God is greater than our hearts and knows everything (1 John 3:20). The Holy Spirit comforts us by attesting that, in spite of our human frailties, we are still children of God (see Romans 8:16). Our deepest identity can only be understood in the light of God's love.

- Where can I find support, comfort, encouragement?
- To understand the role of the Holy Spirit better we must look at the life of Jesus. What Gospel story helps me to understand how God comforts us?

Jesus, our peace, by your Holy Spirit you continue to be for us today what you were for your disciples on earth. In your Gospel you assure us: "I will never leave you alone; I will send the Holy Spirit as a support and a comfort, to remain with you for ever."

The Beauty of God's Love

While he was at Bethany in the house of Simon the leper, as he sat at the table, a woman came with an alabaster jar of very costly ointment of nard, and she broke open the jar and poured the ointment on his head. But some were there who said to one another in anger, "Why was the ointment wasted in this way? For this ointment could have been sold for more than three hundred denarii, and the money given to the poor." And they scolded her. But Jesus said, "Let her alone; why do you trouble her? She has performed a good work for me. For you always have the poor with you, and you can show kindness to them whenever you wish; but you will not always have me. She has done what she could; she has anointed my body beforehand for its burial. Truly I tell you, wherever the good news is proclaimed in the whole world, what she has done will be told in remembrance of her."

– Mark 14:3–9

Adoramus te Christe / *We adore you, Jesus Christ*

A - do - ra - mus te Chri - ste be - ne - di - ci - mus ti - bi,
We a - dore you, Je - sus Christ, and we bless your Ho - ly Name;

qui - a per cru - cem tu - am re - de - mi - sti mun - dum,
tru - ly your cross and pas - sion bring us life and heal - ing,

qui - a per cru - cem tu - am re - de - mi - sti mun - dum.
tru - ly your cross and pas - sion bring us life and heal - ing.

Invited by his friend "Simon the leper" shortly before his Passion, Jesus is in Bethany, a village facing Jerusalem. During the meal, a woman comes up to him with some precious ointment and pours it on his head. This waste disturbs the guests. The ointment cost 300 denarii, a good yearly salary for a worker. That amount of money could have helped many poor people.

Jesus does not agree with those who criticize the woman. And yet nobody can doubt his concern for the poor. "Sell your possessions," he says to those who want to follow him, "and give the money to the poor" (Luke 12:33). Here, too, he says that sharing with the poor will always be necessary. But he wants people to understand that even the most serious moral commitment is in danger of losing its meaning if efficiency becomes the sole criterion. Jesus approves the fact that the woman forgot to calculate and that she was motivated by her love alone. She certainly went beyond what was reasonable, and yet she was right in pouring the perfume on Jesus. Made attentive by her love for him, the Christ, she was the first to honor his crucified body.

Jesus admires the woman's act. He says that in her memory, what she did will be told in the whole world! She has done "a good work," and this could also be translated "a beautiful work." The beauty of this deeply human act reflects the beauty of God's love. God pours out his love for us like this perfume, without calculating or measuring, without conditions. On the eve of his Passion, Christ could recognize himself in this "wasted" ointment. He did not try to save his life; he gave it. "Christ loved us and gave himself up for us" (Ephesians 5:2).

- Would I have seen the woman's act as Simon's guests did, or as Jesus did?
- What helps us to recognize not only the goodness, but also the beauty of God and Christ?
- What can lead us to open our hearts to God and to the poor around us?

Christ, if you ask us, as you did in the Gospel, "Do you love me?", we stammer our reply: "You know that I love you, Christ, perhaps not as I would like to, but I do love you."

An Ever Greater Love

Am I a God near by, says the Lord, and not a God far off? Who can hide in secret places so that I cannot see them? says the Lord. Do I not fill heaven and earth? says the Lord.

– Jeremiah 23:23–24

Confitemini Domino

Give thanks to the Lord for he is good.

"A God who is near": this expression sums up Israel's experience of God's tenderness. God watches over his people, Israel—"shielded him, cared for him, guarded him as the apple of his eye" (Deuteronomy 32:10). But God's people also experienced a "God who is far away," and Jeremiah complains about this: "Why should you be like a stranger in the land?" (Jeremiah 14:8). It is as though God no longer intervened in human affairs; his presence could no longer be felt. He let Jerusalem and its Temple fall into ruin. "I call and you do not answer" (Psalm 22:2). Even those who believe must live as if there were no God.

At that time, some prophets kept on making promises in God's name in order to shore up the morale of the nation. But, in reality, they were inventing them. They felt obliged to fill the vacuum left by the absence of any concrete experience of God. Jeremiah suffered from God's silence, too, but he did not want to pretend. He consented to live with his questions. And one day he received an answer: God is not only "a God who is near" but also "a God who is far away." He is not only found in the experience of fullness, but also in that of lack, of longing. There is no need to fill the vacuum caused by the impression that God is far away, for God "fills heaven and earth" at all times.

The experience of a "God who is far away" gave Jeremiah a deeper understanding of God's love: "The Lord appeared to him from far away. I have loved you with an everlasting love" (31:3). If God seems to hide his face, that is in order to let us discover a love beyond anything we can imagine. If God "flees like the deer" (Saint John of the Cross) and seems far away, that is in order to help us, in our turn, to keep going far along the way of the Gospel.

- How do I react when God seems far away, or even absent?
- To what experiences in my life do the expressions "a God who is near" and "a God who is far away" correspond?
- What helps our love for God to grow?

Jesus, Love of all loving, you were always in me and I had forgotten it. You were in my heart of hearts and I was looking for you elsewhere. When I kept myself far from you, you were waiting for me. And now I dare to tell you: "Christ, you are my life."

23

An Inner Light

[John wrote:] In the beginning was the Word, and the Word was with God, and the Word was God. He was in the beginning with God. All things came into being through him, and without him not one thing came into being. What has come into being in him was life, and the life was the light of all people. The light shines in the darkness, and the darkness has not overcome it. There was a man sent from God, whose name was John. He came as a witness to testify to the light, so that all might believe through him. He himself was not the light, but he came to testify to the light. The true light, which enlightens everyone, was coming into the world. He was in the world, and the world came into being through him; yet the world did not know him. He came to what was his own, and his own people did not accept him. But to all who received him, who believed in his name, he gave power to become children of God.

– John 1:1–12

Jésus le Christ / *Lord Jesus Christ*

Jé - sus le Christ, lu - mière in - té - rieu - re, ne lais - se
Lord Je - sus Christ, your light shines with - in us. Let not my

pas mes té - nè - bres me par - ler. Jé - sus le Christ, lu - mière in - té -
doubts nor my dark - ness speak to me. Lord Je - sus Christ, your light shines with -

rieu - re, don - ne - moi d'ac - cueil - lir ton a - mour. Jé - sus le
in us. Let my heart al - ways wel - come your love. Lord Je - sus

To introduce his Gospel, Saint John confronts us right from the start with the mystery of Christ, presenting him as he will reveal himself in fullness after his resurrection. Jesus manifests himself as the light of the world. Light is something that on the one hand is very powerful (we can think of those rays of light that take billions of years to reach us) but at the same time incredibly fragile, because to block the light all we have to do is to put our hands in front of our eyes. Light and darkness can easily coexist. Light cannot force darkness, but all it takes is the smallest opening for light to be diffused throughout a room.

This light gives life. Not only does it provide warmth and enable us to find our way, but also it situates us in the midst of creation and allows us to discover who God is. Welcoming it means entering the reality of God's life and love, which, in the Resurrection, will show themselves to be stronger than hatred and refusal. Welcoming it also means changing our outlook—no longer wishing to be our own light, no longer wishing at all costs to transform resistances and blind spots by our own powers, but letting in the light that gives new life to what seemed to have become hardened.

We should not be afraid of this call, which seems so demanding—to be a witness to the light, as John the Baptist was, to be ourselves the light of the world, as Jesus invites us to be (see Matthew 5:14). It is not our strength that can achieve this; we need simply to let a reflection of God's love shine through us and radiate outward in the midst of those who are unaware of it.

- What Gospel text helps me understand that Christ is light?
- When I am frightened by darkness, what enables me to realize that Christ's light is near?

God of every human being, you never impose yourself, you never force our heart, but you place your peaceful light within each one of us.

"If You Knew What God Gives"

Jesus came to a Samaritan city called Sychar, near the plot of ground that Jacob had given to his son Joseph. Jacob's well was there, and Jesus, tired out by his journey, was sitting by the well. It was about noon. A Samaritan woman came to draw water, and Jesus said to her, "Give me a drink." (His disciples had gone to the city to buy food.) The Samaritan woman said to him, "How is it that you, a Jew, ask a drink of me, a woman of Samaria?" (Jews do not share things in common with Samaritans.) Jesus answered her, "If you knew the gift of God, and who it is that is saying to you, 'Give me a drink,' you would have asked him, and he would have given you living water." The woman said to him, "Sir, you have no bucket, and the well is deep. Where do you get that living water? Are you greater than our ancestor Jacob, who gave us the well, and with his sons and his flocks drank from it?" Jesus said to her, "Everyone who drinks of this water will be thirsty again, but those who drink of the water that I will give them will never be thirsty. The water that I will give will become in them a spring of water gushing up to eternal life." The woman said to him, "Sir, give me this water, so that I may never be thirsty or have to keep coming here to draw water."

– John 4:5–15

Une soif / Within me my soul is thirsting

U - ne soif em-plit mon â - me: tout a - ban-don-ner en toi le Christ.
With- in me my soul is thirst - ing: to sur - ren-der all in you, O Christ.

Et mon cœur de - meu-re dans l'at-ten - te, tant qu'il ne re - pose en toi.
And my heart with - in is ev - er yearn - ing, un - til it finds rest in you.

26

In a simple meeting by a well, Jesus reveals fully his mission and his identity. According to all the criteria of the surrounding society, the woman who comes to draw water is not a fit person for Jesus to be with. First, she is a Samaritan, a member of a group that for centuries was the hereditary rival of the Jews. Second, she is a woman: her place is neither to converse with a rabbi nor even to speak to a strange man (see 4:27). In addition, she is probably somebody with a bad reputation, a "sinner": she goes out at noon, an hour when she is fairly sure not to meet anybody on the road.

Without hesitating in the least, Jesus enters into a relationship with this undervalued person. By expressing his simple human desire to drink, he shows his esteem for the woman, treating her as an equal or even as someone in a position of superiority, since she has what he needs. Her human dignity is thus fully restored and the foundations of a communion established beyond the boundaries of convention.

This communion is not, however, rooted in a human act of kindness. Although Jesus first appeals to the woman's good will, to the generosity of her heart, this is only a first step toward helping her realize that the most important thing is to receive. He reveals a God who is above all a giver, an overflowing source of life and the only one able to make this source well up. The encounter with Jesus and his request to drink lead the woman to discover her own thirst and to open in her a void that God alone can fill.

- How can we, through simple gestures, create signs of communion that go beyond the barriers of society to respect fully the dignity of others?
- What helps me to open myself to the gift of God, to remember that God only asks something of me in order to give me still more?

Risen Jesus, at times you see us bewildered, like strangers on this earth. But our souls are filled by a thirst, a longing for your presence. And our hearts finds no rest until they can lay down in you, Christ, what was keeping us far from you.

Entering a Life of Communion

Now before the festival of the Passover, Jesus knew that his hour had come to depart from this world and go to the Father. Having loved his own who were in the world, he loved them to the end. The devil had already put it into the heart of Judas, son of Simon Iscariot, to betray him. And during supper Jesus, knowing that the Father had given all things into his hands, and that he had come from God and was going to God, got up from the table, took off his outer robe, and tied a towel around himself. Then he poured water into a basin and began to wash the disciples' feet and to wipe them with the towel that was tied around him. He came to Simon Peter, who said to him, "Lord, are you going to wash my feet?" Jesus answered, "You do not know now what I am doing, but later you will understand." Peter said to him, "You will never wash my feet." Jesus answered, "Unless I wash you, you have no share with me." Simon Peter said to him, "Lord, not my feet only but also my hands and my head!" Jesus said to him, "One who has bathed does not need to wash, except for the feet, but is entirely clean. And you are clean, though not all of you." For he knew who was to betray him; for this reason he said, "Not all of you are clean." After he had washed their feet, had put on his robe, and had returned to the table, he said to them, "Do you know what I have done to you? You call me Teacher and Lord—and you are right, for that is what I am. So if I, your Lord and Teacher, have washed your feet, you also ought to wash one another's feet. For I have set you an example, that you also should do as I have done to you. Very truly, I tell you, servants are not greater than their master, nor are messengers greater than the one who sent them. If you know these things, you are blessed if you do them."

– John 13:1–17

Ubi caritas

U-bi ca-ri-tas et a - mor, u-bi ca-ri-tas De-us i - bi est.

Where there is charity and love, God is to be found.

28

In Jesus' last meal with his disciples, Saint John's Gospel emphasizes the episode of the foot washing. In those days, it was customary to bring water when guests entered a house so that they could wash their feet. The slaves, who brought them a basin of water and a towel, would sometimes do it for them. On exceptional occasions, a member of the family could perform the act, to honor a special guest.

When Jesus washes the disciples' feet, he upsets the customary order of things. He takes the place of a servant. He honors his disciples. Curiously, he washes their feet "during the meal" when they are already lying on couches, and not when they enter the room. Was this to make up for something forgotten? In any case, doing it then gives the act an even greater symbolic power. It is a parable in act whose meaning has to be "understood" (vv. 7 and 12).

Washing feet normally indicates a transition, going from outside the home to inside. Christ's act also indicates a transition—the disciples' entry into a new type of relationship with him and among themselves. Jesus is so insistent in the face of Peter's refusal because communion with him is at stake. "Unless I wash you, you have no share with me" (v. 8). This participation with Christ involves a twofold transformation. Jesus, the master, becomes a servant. And the disciples are transformed into friends (see also John 15:13–15).

In order to love with Christ, to "do what he has done to us" (v. 15), we need to let his love change us. Christ loves me to the point of serving me and taking my place, and I have to let him take care of all my cares. And then, just as between friends, we will share everything in common. He takes my sin as his own. And his treasure of love becomes mine, so that I can draw from it in order to love to the very end.

- Why does Peter resist so much when Jesus wants to wash his feet?
- What does it mean for me to welcome Christ's love?
- What needs to change in our relationship with one another as Christians? How can we follow Christ's example?

Jesus, our hope, enable us to hear your voice when you say to us: "I, Christ, love you." That is a source of peace for our hearts.

TO THE WELLSPRINGS OF FORGIVENESS

"I Do Not Condemn You"

The scribes and the Pharisees brought a woman who had been caught in adultery; and making her stand before all of them, they said to Jesus, "Teacher, this woman was caught in the very act of committing adultery. Now in the law Moses commanded us to stone such women. Now what do you say?" They said this to test him, so that they might have some charge to bring against him. Jesus bent down and wrote with his finger on the ground. When they kept on questioning him, he straightened up and said to them, "Let anyone among you who is without sin be the first to throw a stone at her." And once again he bent down and wrote on the ground. When they heard it, they went away, one by one, beginning with the elders; and Jesus was left alone with the woman standing before him. Jesus straightened up and said to her, "Woman, where are they? Has no one condemned you?" She said, "No one, sir." And Jesus said, "Neither do I condemn you. Go your way, and from now on do not sin again."

– John 8:3–11

Bóg jest miłością / *God is forgiveness*

God is for-give-ness. Dare to for-give and God will be with you.

God is for-give-ness. Love and do not fear.

Jesus' first words in Mark's Gospel are: "The time is fulfilled and the kingdom of God has come near; repent, and believe in the good news" (Mark 1:14). A key word in this passage is *metanoia,* usually translated "repent" or "be converted." *Metanoia* signifies, first of all, a "change of mentality." This change of mentality is necessary to open our hearts and to welcome the kingdom of God, God's presence in our lives.

The story of the woman who had been caught in adultery is a good example of this change of mentality and of heart. It shows how our horizon can be transformed so that we look at our lives in the light of the gospel, in the same way that God looks at our lives.

In this story, we see that Jesus doesn't react the way the crowd does to the mystery of human weakness. The crowd and the Pharisees see one single incident in the life of this woman. Jesus, who knows the hearts of all those he meets, sees much more. He sees the entire person, the truth. He knows that there is more in this woman than that which has just taken place. Jesus believes that human beings can be transformed. By not adding his voice to the voices that condemn the woman, he opens a path: "I came not to judge the world, but to save the world" (John 12:47). Welcomed just as she is, with her gifts and her limitations, this woman can go away, take responsibility for her life, and love others just as she has been shown love. The woman who had been surrounded by death has come back to life.

Today, it is rare for someone to be treated as the woman was in this story. But there are many other voices, a whole inner darkness that accuses us: "You are guilty." What then would it mean to turn toward the light of the Gospel (*metanoia*)?

- After having read this story, what surprises you?
- How do you understand Christ's way of looking at others?

Jesus of mercy, you invite us to be in communion with you. And our hearts rejoice when we realize that no one is excluded either from your forgiveness or your love.

Entering the Joy of God's Forgiveness

Jesus said, "There was a man who had two sons. The younger of them said to his father, 'Father, give me the share of the property that will belong to me.' So he divided his property between them. A few days later the younger son gathered all he had and travelled to a distant country, and there he squandered his property in dissolute living. When he had spent everything, a severe famine took place throughout that country, and he began to be in need. So he went and hired himself out to one of the citizens of that country, who sent him to his fields to feed the pigs. He would gladly have filled himself with the pods that the pigs were eating; and no one gave him anything. But when he came to himself he said, 'How many of my father's hired hands have bread enough and to spare, but here I am dying of hunger! I will get up and go to my father, and I will say to him, "Father, I have sinned against heaven and before you; I am no longer worthy to be called your son; treat me like one of your hired hands."' So he set off and went to his father. But while he was still far off, his father saw him and was filled with compassion; he ran and put his arms around him and kissed him. Then the son said to him, 'Father, I have sinned against heaven and before you; I am no longer worthy to be called your son.' But the father said to his slaves, 'Quickly, bring out a robe—the best one—and put it on him; put a ring on his finger and sandals on his feet. And get the fatted calf and kill it, and let us eat and celebrate; for this son of mine was dead and is alive again; he was lost and is found!' And they began to celebrate."

– Luke 15:11–32

Misericordias Domini

Mi - se - ri - cor - di - as Do - mi - ni in æ - ter - num can - ta - bo.

I will sing forever the mercy of God.

Saint Augustine offered the following commentary on the parable of the father who welcomes his son, relating it to Jesus' words in Matthew 11:28–30:

> While the prodigal son was still thinking about what he would say to his father,... his father ran to meet him. What does that mean, to run to meet him, but to assure him of his mercy in advance? "While he was still far off, his father ran to meet him, moved by pity." Why was he moved by pity? Because his son was miserable. "He ran to meet him and threw himself on his neck," in other words, he put his arm around his neck.
>
> The Father's arm is the Son; he gave his son Christ to bear; that burden is not a heavy weight; rather, it offers relief. "My yoke is easy and my burden light" (Matthew 11:30). He put his weight on his son, who had stood up, and in putting his weight on him he did not let him fall down again. Christ's yoke is so light that not only is it not a burden, but it offers relief. It is not light in the sense that we say some burdens are light because, although they do have a certain weight, they do not weigh as much as others:... Christ's burden is not like that; you have to bear it in order to find relief; if you set it down, you will be more burdened... So when the father fell on his son's neck, he did not burden him; he honored him; he was not a heavy weight. For how could anyone be able to carry God, unless the God he carried carried him?

- How can we not remain trapped in self-reproach, but fix our eyes on the Father who runs to meet us?
- When, in my life, have I experienced Christ as an arm around my neck?

God of mercy, you never stop searching for all who have distanced themselves from you. And by your forgiveness, you call us to sing: a thirst fills my soul, a thirst to surrender everything in you.

Entering the Joy of God's Forgiveness (continued)

Jesus continued his story: "Now his elder son was in the field; and when he came and approached the house, he heard music and dancing. He called one of the slaves and asked what was going on. He replied, 'Your brother has come, and your father has killed the fatted calf, because he has got him back safe and sound.' Then he became angry and refused to go in. His father came out and began to plead with him. But he answered his father, 'Listen! For all these years I have been working like a slave for you, and I have never disobeyed your command; yet you have never given me even a young goat so that I might celebrate with my friends. But when this son of yours came back, who has devoured your property with prostitutes, you killed the fatted calf for him!' Then the father said to him, 'Son, you are always with me, and all that is mine is yours. But we had to celebrate and rejoice, because this brother of yours was dead and has come to life; he was lost and has been found.'"

– Luke 15:11–32

Dona nobis pacem

Grant us peace of heart.

If the heart of the "parable of the father" is the father's welcome of his son who comes home (see vv. 20–24), the climax of the parable is the father's reply to his elder son. We should be thankful to the older son for having merited that unparalleled response! If the parable had concluded with the unexpected welcome shown to the younger son, we could have thought that the father had not fully shown all of himself as he was. His reply to the older brother, however, makes it evident that this is what the father is truly like. This is his deepest being, his "all" that he wants to share with us, and he awaits our response.

The father does not get angry with his elder son. He does not argue with him, either. Instead, he speaks to him words full of affection. "My child." That is more affectionate than "my son." There is no criticism or accusation regarding the son's bitter reproaches. The father does not defend himself. On the contrary, the father does not waste any time evaluating his own behavior or that of his elder son, emphasizing instead the intimate, unique relationship he has with his son: "You are always with me." Their relationship has not changed. Whereas the son spoke in terms of "me" (v. 29), the father places the accent on "you."

This father has no desire to win a victory over anybody. He simply believed that the elder brother, seeing the love he had for his younger brother, would realize that he is loved in the same way, and that he would then love in the same way. The father remains patient and kind, but at the same time makes no concessions. His "norm," his "law," is unchangeable. He says that they *had to* celebrate and rejoice. The elder son had said, "your son" (v. 30), that ne'er-do-well, but the father replies: "No, he's your brother. You can begin anew the relationship you had with him." The older son had said, "But he lived with loose women!" "He was dead and came back to life," the father replied. "He was lost and now is found!" Once again, the father repeats his song (see v. 24). It's like a refrain; he sings it over and over in his heart. The father is overflowing with joy and gratefulness. Nothing can take that gladness away from him, not even his elder son's bad mood.

- What is typical of the way in which the father rejoices, loves, and shares?
- Why does the parable not tell us how the older son replied?
- How can I go toward those who have wounded me?

Holy Spirit, mystery of a presence, you bathe us in unfailing kindness. It allows a life of humble trusting to blossom in us... And our hearts become lighter.

Do Not Cling to Sadness

Jesus went out and saw a tax collector named Levi sitting at the tax booth; and he said to him, "Follow me." And he got up, left everything, and followed him. Then Levi gave a great banquet for him in his house; and there was a large crowd of tax collectors and others sitting at the table with them. The Pharisees and their scribes were complaining to his disciples, saying, "Why do you eat and drink with tax collectors and sinners?" Jesus answered, "Those who are well have no need of a physician, but those who are sick; I have come to call not the righteous but sinners to repentance."

– Luke 5:27–32

Magnificat (canon)

Sing out my soul.

Levi the tax collector, a more-or-less honest collaborator with the occupying power, was certainly not well loved. And he must even have had a certain aversion for himself, seeing that the profits from his dishonesty did not compensate for the lack of real friends. In this existence heading for failure, Jesus sees something deeper. Behind the visible reality, there is generosity, the desire to live for an absolute. Jesus already sees in Levi a good heart capable of great things. So Jesus says to him, "I trust in you. Come with me. You can be my friend, my witness." And Levi does not ask himself if he is ready. Immediately, with no hesitation, he stands up, and his joy is so great that he shares it at once, organizing a party to which he invites many people who could think they were far from God. He experiences "a reorientation of mind and heart."

That is what "conversion" or "repentance" means: discovering that Christ trusts me, leaving behind my isolation and my soul-destroying sadness, standing up, trusting that I can do something for the joy of others. Jesus relates conversion to healing. When we are seriously ill, we cannot heal ourselves, yet no one is healed against his or her will. This is also true of conversion: like forgiveness, God gives it to us (see Acts 5:31). It is up to us not to cling to our sadness.

- What did Levi discover in his encounter with Christ that caused him to get up quickly and organize a celebration?
- Where do I welcome God's love? In prayer, in some words from the Gospel, in the Eucharist? Through the trust that someone shows me, or in the concern I have for others?
- How can I share joy with those around me?

Jesus, hope of our hearts, when we realize that your love is above all forgiveness, something in us is soothed and even transformed. We ask you: "What do you want from me?" And by the Holy Spirit you reply: "Let nothing trouble you; dare to give your life."

No One Is Excluded

Jesus said, "The kingdom of heaven is like a landowner who went out early in the morning to hire laborers for his vineyard. After agreeing with the laborers for the usual daily wage, he sent them into his vineyard. When he went out about nine o'clock, he saw others standing idle in the marketplace; and he said to them, 'You also go into the vineyard, and I will pay you whatever is right.' So they went. When he went out again about noon and about three o'clock, he did the same. And about five o'clock he went out and found others standing around; and he said to them, 'Why are you standing here idle all day?' They said to him, 'Because no one has hired us.' He said to them, 'You also go into the vineyard.' When evening came, the owner of the vineyard said to his manager, 'Call the laborers and give them their pay, beginning with the last and then going to the first.' When those hired about five o'clock came, each of them received the usual daily wage. Now when the first came, they thought they would receive more; but each of them also received the usual daily wage. And when they received it, they grumbled against the landowner, saying, 'These last worked only one hour, and you have made them equal to us who have borne the burden of the day and the scorching heat.' But he replied to one of them, 'Friend, I am doing you no wrong; did you not agree with me for the usual daily wage? Take what belongs to you and go; I choose to give to this last the same as I give to you. Am I not allowed to do what I choose with what belongs to me? Or are you envious because I am generous?'"

– Matthew 20:1–15

Dona la pace / *Dyro dangnefedd*

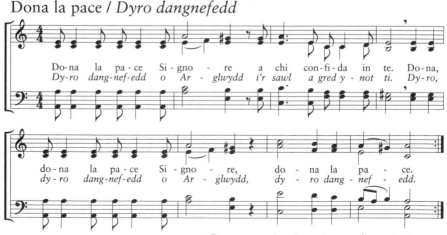

Give peace, Lord, to those who trust in you.

John, known as Chrysostom, "golden mouth," lived for a few years as a hermit before becoming a priest, and then bishop of Constantinople at the end of the fourth century. In a meditation for the feast of Easter, he invites everyone to be joyful, taking up the Gospel parable:

> Let those who live their faith, those who love the Lord, come to taste the enchantment of this feast! Let the faithful servants enter, full of gladness, into their master's joy. Let those who have borne the weight of fasting come and receive their salary.
>
> Those who began their work at the first hour will receive their just wages today. Those who came at the third hour will rejoice with thanksgiving. Those who will only arrive at the sixth hour can approach without fear; they will not be deprived. If some have lingered until the ninth hour, they can come without hesitation. The workers of the eleventh hour will not suffer for their delay.
>
> For the Lord is generous: he receives the last just as the first; he grants rest to the workers of the eleventh hour just as to those who began their work at dawn. He shows mercy to the last and fills the first; he gives to the former without forgetting the latter; he does not only consider the work, but already grasps the intention…
>
> Let no one lament his poverty: the kingdom is open to all. Let no one weep over his sins: forgiveness has risen from the tomb. Let no one fear death: the Lord's death has freed us; he brought down death when it kept him in chains.

- How can we, too, enter into this joy and realize that nothing in our lives is excluded from the joy of the Resurrection?
- In what situations do I need to remember this forgiveness and this liberation?

Christ of compassion, through your Gospel we discover that measuring what we are or what we are not leads nowhere. What matters is the humble trusting of faith. By it we are led to understand that "all God can do is give his love."

Nothing Can Separate Us from God's Love

"The days are surely coming, says the Lord, when I will make a new covenant with the house of Israel and the house of Judah. It will not be like the covenant that I made with their ancestors when I took them by the hand to bring them out of the land of Egypt—covenant that they broke, though I was their husband, says the Lord. But this is the covenant that I will make with the house of Israel after those days, says the Lord: I will put my law within them, and I will write it on their hearts; and I will be their God, and they shall be my people. No longer shall they teach one another, or say to each other, 'Know the Lord,' for they shall all know me, from the least of them to the greatest, says the Lord; for I will forgive their iniquity, and remember their sin no more."
– Jeremiah 31:31–34

Nothing can ever

Noth-ing can ev-er come be-tween us and the love of God,

the love of God re-vealed to us in Christ Je - sus.

Throughout the Bible, God reveals himself as the one who offers to make a "covenant," to watch over his people and to choose them as witnesses to his love and faithfulness. In this context, the "Law" is not an obligation. It is, above all, a gift that recalls the covenant and shows the people the limits they must not cross so that the covenant may be lived out to the full.

In the prophecy of Jeremiah, we sense God's deep joy that announces the renewal of his covenant, but in such a way that nothing can ever destroy it again. The sign of this covenant will no longer be outward; it will be an intimate presence in the depths of the heart. How can we not think of the confident words of Saint Paul, "I am convinced that... nothing will be able to separate us from the love of God in Christ Jesus our Lord" (Romans 8:38–39)?

Fifty days after Passover, at the time when the Jewish people were celebrating the gift of the Law on Sinai, the apostles experienced the gift of the Holy Spirit, who "poured God's love into our hearts" (Romans 5:5). This presence promised by Jesus—"the Spirit of truth will guide you into all the truth" (John 16:13)—fulfills the prophecy of Jeremiah. "They shall all know me, from the least of them to the greatest, for I shall forgive their iniquity..." (Jeremiah 31:34). Is not the Holy Spirit given to remind us, day after day, that forgiveness is always possible?

- What changes for me when I remember that God offers me a covenant relationship?
- What words of God are "written on my heart," set in the depths of my being?

God of mercy, when we understand that nothing can separate us from you, trust in you opens for us the road that leads upward toward a peace-filled joy.

A Covenant Based on Forgiveness

I will sprinkle clean water upon you, and you shall be clean from all your uncleannesses, and from all your idols I will cleanse you. A new heart I will give you, and a new spirit I will put within you; and I will remove from your body the heart of stone and give you a heart of flesh. I will put my spirit within you, and make you follow my statutes and be careful to observe my ordinances. Then you shall live in the land that I gave to your ancestors; and you shall be my people, and I will be your God.

– Ezekiel 36:25–28

Ostende nobis (canon)

Show us, Lord, your mercy; come soon.

Sent into exile in Babylon, Ezekiel received the calling to communicate God's word in the face of the indifference and the apathy of his people who, having lost all their hope, were "impudent and stubborn" (2:4). Instead of requiring Israel to change in order to be worthy of him, God makes a commitment by taking the initiative. By his forgiveness, God will purify his people and remove their "heart of stone." He will do it in such a way that nothing remains of the misfortunes and mistakes of the past, making sure that nothing is opposed to God's presence among his people and in their heart, which has become a "heart of flesh."

God will put his "spirit" in them. God himself will dwell in believers' hearts. The Breath of Life, the Spirit of God will renew them from within and will animate them as the principle of their life and behavior. In this way, each person will be able to follow the law, the expression of God's will, faithfully. In this intimate communion with God, human will and activity are henceforth to be perfectly conformed to the divine will. That is the new covenant offered by God to his people, and to each believer.

This new covenant is based on forgiveness. God's forgiveness is total, irrevocable. The past is wiped away. God does not want to remember our sins any longer (see Jeremiah 31:34b), so we, too, do not have to be tormented by them. In this way we can escape from the burden of the past. Liberated from remorse, from guilty feelings, from a focus on ourselves, from remaining at a standstill, we are enabled henceforth to create in communion. The forgiveness offered at every moment brings new life to us. However serious our wrongdoing was, a new beginning is always possible. The harshness that hurt others and ourselves can be transformed into a source of life.

When the disciples experienced this newness in a radical way at Pentecost, they understood that this promise was meant for all and that, by the overflowing gift of his Spirit, the risen Christ made a new communion possible.

- When have I been made aware of the "heart of stone" in me?
- What does it mean to say that "God removes the heart of stone in us and replaces it with a heart of flesh"?
- How or when in my daily life can I let the life-giving Spirit act within me?

God of all eternity, open in us the gates of your mercy. And we understand that the will of your love is not a law written on tablets of stone. It consists of burning charity, written in our hearts.

45

Transformed Because Forgiven

When the day of Pentecost had come, they were all together in one place. And suddenly from heaven there came a sound like the rush of a violent wind, and it filled the entire house where they were sitting. Divided tongues, as of fire, appeared among them, and a tongue rested on each of them. All of them were filled with the Holy Spirit and began to speak in other languages, as the Spirit gave them ability...

Peter said, "This Jesus God raised up, and of that all of us are witnesses. Being therefore exalted at the right hand of God, and having received from the Father the promise of the Holy Spirit, he has poured out this that you both see and hear. For David did not ascend into the heavens, but he himself says, 'The Lord said to my Lord, "Sit at my right hand, until I make your enemies your footstool."' Therefore let the entire house of Israel know with certainty that God has made him both Lord and Messiah, this Jesus whom you crucified."

– Acts 2:1–4, 32–36

Esprit consolateur

Consoling Spirit, love of all love.

"Peter, standing with the Eleven, raised his voice and addressed them" (Acts 2:14). The inhabitants of Jerusalem must have thought that the disciples of the crucified Jesus had been broken by the striking failure of their master, that they had become bitter or filled with the violence of the desperate. What a surprise to discover men on their feet who leave their hiding place and come to meet them with free and open hearts, people with words of confidence and reconciliation on their lips, eager to share what has changed their lives: an encounter with the risen Christ, with his peace and his forgiveness.

Having recognized the risen Lord, the apostles are without plans for the future and without regrets. The risen Christ has visited them and filled them with his Spirit. This Spirit is the defender that Jesus had promised—the Spirit of forgiveness, peace, joy, strength and boldness. The miracle of tongues is the seed of a communion that overturns barriers of every sort.

The apostles do not keep for themselves what they have received. With Peter they proclaim, "The promise is for you, for your children, and for all who are far away..." (Acts 2:39). On the rock of the Spirit of the risen Christ, the kingdom of God is being built, visible and accessible in the communion of the Church. The risen Lord founds the Church on his forgiveness. It will be a visible expression of his being in the world.

- How can I bear witness to this twofold "Pentecost opening of doors": going toward others to communicate Christ and welcoming them more broadly into my own community?
- What recent events, what persons I have met, have been for me bearers of the power and the creative liberty of forgiveness?

Holy Spirit, you make it possible for us to cross the deserts of the heart. By your forgiveness, "you dissipate our faults like the morning mist." There we find Christian freedom; there lies the wonder of a love.

"Forgive Them; They Do Not Know What They Are Doing"

> *When they came to the place that is called The Skull, they crucified Jesus there with the criminals, one on his right and one on his left. Then Jesus said, "Father, forgive them; for they do not know what they are doing." And they cast lots to divide his clothing.*
>
> – Luke 23:33–34

Bleibet hier / *Stay with me*

From the time he joined penitents going to John the Baptist to receive a baptism of repentance, Jesus entered into solidarity with sinners and those aware of their poverty before God. He committed his entire life to manifest the good news to them. Now he has no place on earth to live. After having been abandoned and denied by his disciples, condemned by the country's highest authorities, rejected by the people, he is nailed to a cross: the death reserved for slaves and criminals.

Yet he does not pay attention to this scandal, or to the evil that is done to him. He does not complain about the suffering he undergoes. He does not think about the questions: "Why this unjustified evil? Who is responsible for it?" His main preoccupation is saving a relationship with each person. He does not imprison anyone in the evil that has been done. He believes in them more than they do in themselves. By this forgiveness, reconciliation is already offered. It is in the peace and the light of the Resurrection that this will gradually become accessible.

When we pass through an inexplicable trial, when we feel forsaken by those in whom we had placed our trust, we can be surprised to find a violent reaction welling up in us. Sometimes we feel the need to get some distance, to allow some time to pass. Then we realize that forgiveness is not a natural attitude for human beings. But in such moments of crisis we can also discover that living a life of forgiveness means first and foremost letting the risen Christ forgive within us.

All who choose to let Christ pray in them "Father, forgive" remain free of violence and bitterness. Free of distances, of an indifference that gives the illusion of protecting them, like armor, against a suffering that has become too unbearable. The heart remains alive; it can begin to hope anew.

- For what person or situation can I call upon Christ's forgiveness?
- What road to the future does forgiveness open for me? With whom? How does forgiveness enable us to create something with others over time?
- What other words or parables of Jesus help me to root myself in his forgiveness?

Christ Jesus, you did not come to earth to condemn the world but so that through you, the risen Lord, every human being might find a path of communion. And when love goes to the point of forgiving, the heart, even when beset by trials, begins to live anew.

Living as Reconciled People

Jesus said, "I came that they may have life, and have it abundantly. I am the good shepherd. The good shepherd lays down his life for the sheep. The hired hand, who is not the shepherd and does not own the sheep, sees the wolf coming and leaves the sheep and runs away—and the wolf snatches them and scatters them. The hired hand runs away because a hired hand does not care for the sheep. I am the good shepherd. I know my own and my own know me, just as the Father knows me and I know the Father. And I lay down my life for the sheep. I have other sheep that do not belong to this fold. I must bring them also, and they will listen to my voice. So there will be one flock, one shepherd."

– John 10:10b–16

In te confido / *Christ of compassion*

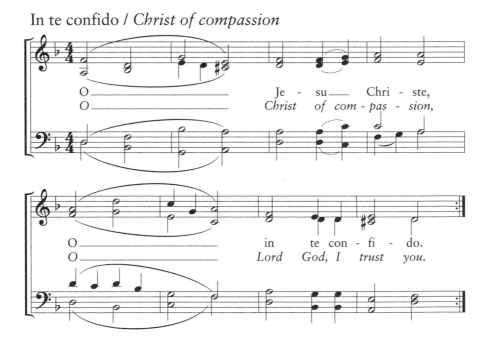

Like a shepherd, Christ accomplishes a twofold task: he takes care of each one, and he brings all together. He gives the fullness of life to each one in particular, not neglecting anyone, even those who get lost; he does not punish them but rather does all he can to find them. And to gather together into a communion, he centers his teaching on mutual love. On the cross, when apparently he can do nothing, he continues to gather by refusing to view those who torture him as enemies. Risen from the dead, he is completely without limits: like a shepherd looking for lost sheep, he goes toward every human being, no matter how far from God they seem to be.

The shepherd gathers; the wolf disperses in order to destroy. The bitterness of humiliations and wounds that were never forgiven, of hatred and violent oppositions, are like wolves that disperse and tear apart the life of communion Christ has brought. In the face of divisions, Christ did not flee; he remained present even at the heart of the strongest tensions. "He put hostility to death," says Saint Paul (Ephesians 2:16). Not by an act of force, but by loving and forgiving those who mistreated him.

In the image of Christ, each of us is called to bring together and to say no to what divides. Taking risks to avoid or heal divisions (between family members, nations, Christians of the same town) is a way of sharing in the mission of the Good Shepherd according to our own possibilities.

- How can I always remain close to the source of a love that forgives?
- Who does God entrust to me so that we can live together day after day as reconciled people?

God of all loving, you love and search for each of us even before we loved you. And we are seized with wonder to discover that you look upon every human being with infinite tenderness and deep compassion.

TOWARD AN INNER HEALING

From Distress to Praise

With my voice I cry to the Lord;
with my voice I make supplication to the Lord.
I pour out my complaint before him;
I tell my trouble before him.
When my spirit is faint,
you know my way.
In the path where I walk
they have hidden a trap for me.
Look on my right hand and see –
there is no one who takes notice of me;
no refuge remains to me;
no one cares for me.
I cry to you, O Lord;
I say, "You are my refuge,
my portion in the land of the living."
Give heed to my cry,
for I am brought very low.
Save me from my persecutors,
for they are too strong for me.
Bring me out of prison,
so that I may give thanks to your name.
The righteous will surround me,
for you will deal bountifully with me.

— Psalm 142:1–7

Dans nos obscurités / *Within our darkest night*

Within our darkest night, you kindle the fire that never dies away.

Psalm 142 is the prayer of a poor person; it was the favorite psalm of Saint Francis. It traces out a road that goes from lament to praise, from solitude to communion. From the depths of their distress, those who pray the psalm "pour forth" their lament, accepting that the retaining walls within will break down. The soul holds nothing back; it lets its pain and confusion flow out freely before God. This distress is caused in part by the harshness of others, by "persecutors." But still worse is the solitude, the total absence of comprehension and of concern: "there is no one who takes notice of me; no one cares for me" (v. 5). Those who were close have disappeared.

Then the lamentation becomes prayer, a humble request for liberation by God. And prayer causes a taste for life to return. Saying to God, "you are my portion in the land of the living" (v. 6) means refusing to despair, it means continuing to search for happiness on this earth, in spite of bitter disappointments. In prayer, I have the assurance that I will sing again. Made free, I will give thanks.

Praise brings us out of solitude and into communion. I thank God for a gift, and I escape from my isolation. A gift received from God overflows and spreads out. When I am filled, I become a seed of communion. I become hospitable: "The righteous will surround me, for you will deal bountifully with me" (v. 8). Filled with the happiness that comes from God, I will not refuse to share my joy with anyone, even with those who previously ignored or despised me.

- What disappointments have I experienced that could cause me to withdraw into myself?
- How is trust in God expressed in this psalm?
- What gift have I received from God that I can share with others? With whom can I live in communion through a shared joy?

Christ Jesus, you never lead us into discouragements that knock us off balance, but you enable us to achieve a communion with you. And though there may be trials in store for each person, there is above all a compassion that comes from you. It brings us back to life.

From Darkness toward the Light

How long, O Lord? Will you forget me forever?
How long will you hide your face from me?
How long must I bear pain in my soul,
and have sorrow in my heart all day long?
How long shall my enemy be exalted over me?
Consider and answer me, O Lord my God!
Give light to my eyes, or I will sleep the sleep of death,
and my enemy will say, "I have prevailed";
my foes will rejoice because I am shaken.
But I trusted in your steadfast love;
my heart shall rejoice in your salvation.
I will sing to the Lord,
because he has dealt bountifully with me.

– Psalm 13

La ténèbre / *Our darkness*

La té - nè - bre n'est point té - nè - bre de - vant toi: la
Our_ dark - ness is nev - er dark - ness in your sight: the

nuit com - me le jour est lu - miè - re. La té -
*deep - est night is clear as the day - light. Our_*

One of the most beautiful aspects of the Book of Psalms is the frankness with which believers express to God all that is in them. Far from limiting themselves to edifying thoughts, the authors of the psalms cast all their pain and their despair before God, without sorting out in advance what is acceptable and what is not. This freedom in prayer testifies to an impressive trust in God, even in the middle of the night, and already carries with it the seeds of a new dawn.

The author of this psalm sees himself at the bottom of a well, trapped in a suffering that seems unending. What causes his distress, more than this or that particular misfortune, is the impression that God has abandoned him. Since he no longer feels God's presence, he is left all alone with those inner voices that come from "the enemy," which bring him closer and closer to despair. That is the meaning of the word "revolt" (v. 3a): those obsessive thoughts that try and convince us that God no longer loves us, that in fact we deserve our atrocious fate.

But then, instead of "letting his darkness speak to him" (St. Augustine), the psalmist makes a leap of trust and lifts up his groaning to God. From the depths of his darkness, he remembers God's faithful love for him. He makes a choice, refusing to consent to the victory of the enemy. And as a result, a new beginning is made possible; a small space opens up, large enough for God to rush in, and the lament can turn into a song of praise for a rediscovered communion.

- Where can I find the trust to express in prayer everything that is in me, without wearing any masks in God's presence?
- What Bible texts can be helpful when "the enemy" tries to separate me from God's love?
- What enables me to keep awake instead of shutting my eyes out of fear or routine?

God of all loving, why should we wait for our hearts to be changed in order to go to you? You transfigure them. In our wounds themselves you enable a communion with you to grow. And the gates of praise open within us.

Plans for Welfare and Not for Harm

Then Job answered the Lord: "I know that you can do all things, and that no purpose of yours can be thwarted. Who is this that hides counsel without knowledge? Therefore I have uttered what I did not understand, things too wonderful for me, which I did not know. Hear, and I will speak; I will question you, and you declare to me. I had heard of you by the hearing of the ear, but now my eye sees you; therefore I despise myself, and repent in dust and ashes."

– Job 42:1–6

De noche / *By night we hasten*

De no - che_i - re - mos, de no - che que
By night, we has - ten, in dark - ness, to

pa - ra_en con - trar la fuen - te, só - lo la sed nos a -
search for— liv - ing wa - ter, on - ly our thirst leads us

lum - bra, só - lo la sed nos a - lum - bra. De
on - ward, on - ly our thirst leads us on - ward. By

The Book of Job directly confronts the question that has always unsettled people's minds and kept many from believing in a God of love. Why does God allow innocent people to suffer? A figure of all the good persons who have become victimized by evil, Job does his best to keep going in a situation in which there seems to be no way out. An honest man, he refuses to consent to the too-facile explanations with which his friends attempt to comfort him. In his distress, he even reaches the point of concluding that human beings are unable to understand a God whose ways are so disconcerting. Life on this earth seems destined to remain an enigma: "Where shall wisdom be found?...Mortals do not know the way to it, and it is not found in the land of the living...It is hidden from the eyes of all living" (Job 28:12a, 13, 21a).

Then, when all hope seems to have vanished once and for all, God himself enters the picture. After encountering him, Job speaks these words of light: "I had heard of you by the hearing of the ear, but now my eye sees you." The answer to the question that haunts him is not an intellectual one. Job does not discover any clever arguments that "explain" his situation. At the heart of his suffering, however, he has an experience of God that changes radically his way of looking at things. The trials he suffered have brought him closer to the living God who, beyond our preconceived ideas, "forms plans for your welfare and not for harm, to give you a future with hope" (see Jeremiah 29:11). His painful experience has removed a veil and enabled him to discover that, although the Lord is different from anything he had imagined and his ways are often almost incomprehensible, God is not his enemy. On the contrary, God is the one who constantly calls us to leave behind our too-human certainties in order to find peace in a communion with him.

- Have I gone through times of trial when my habitual way of viewing myself, God, and the world was called into question and no longer worked? What enabled me to find my balance again?
- Have I had the experience that God is always beyond all the images we have of him? When and how?

Bless us, Christ Jesus: you come to comfort our hearts when the incomprehensible happens—the suffering of the innocent.

"Do Not Let Your Hearts Be Troubled or Afraid!"

Jesus said to his disciples, "Peace I leave with you; my peace I give to you. I do not give to you as the world gives. Do not let your hearts be troubled, and do not let them be afraid."

– John 14:27

Mon âme se repose / *In God alone*

Each time a personal trial or a crisis concerning the human family arises, whether serious illness, natural disaster, conflict, or violence, we are disconcerted. Our plans are upset; our outlook and even our identity can be called into question. The idea we have of the world and our own lives is at stake, and we are beset by worry: what if the misfortune were to continue? In such a situation, what is the peace Christ gives?

Let us remember Elijah's discovery on Mount Horeb (see 1 Kings 19:11–14): God was not in the fire, nor in the earthquake, nor in the hurricane, but in the murmur of silence. In order to discover how God calls us to deal with things, we first need to find our way to this silence. We need to still the voices that play upon our fears and pass beyond the images of violence, suffering, and anger, which can so easily monopolize our attention.

Jesus gives peace by reassuring us that the bond with him will remain, whatever our fears. After his resurrection he even says, "Peace be with you. As the Father has sent me, so I send you" (John 20:21).

In the face of the fears I have of losing myself, with the limits and doubts that are mine, it is only natural to want to withdraw and protect myself. But even though I feel myself completely incapable of being "sent out," and this call to give of myself takes me out of my depth, there is, nevertheless, deep down within me, a longing to follow in the footsteps of Christ.

- How does Christ the servant truly set me free from my fears?
- When have I discovered the way in which he looks at situations and persons?
- What does it mean to share in the universal heart of Christ and to be a bearer of urgent good news for all human beings?

Jesus, light of our hearts, since you rose from the dead, by the Holy Spirit you have never stopped coming to us. At whatever point we may be, you are always waiting for us. And you tell us: come to me, you who are overburdened, and you will find relief.

With Us Even in Trials

Now on that same day two of them were going to a village called Emmaus, about seven miles from Jerusalem, and talking with each other about all these things that had happened. While they were talking and discussing, Jesus himself came near and went with them, but their eyes were kept from recognizing him. And he said to them, "What are you discussing with each other while you walk along?" They stood still, looking sad. Then one of them, whose name was Cleopas, answered him, "Are you the only stranger in Jerusalem who does not know the things that have taken place there in these days?" He asked them, "What things?" They replied, "The things about Jesus of Nazareth, who was a prophet mighty in deed and word before God and all the people, and how our chief priests and leaders handed him over to be condemned to death and crucified him. But we had hoped that he was the one to redeem Israel. Yes, and besides all this, it is now the third day since these things took place."… Then he said to them, "Oh, how foolish you are, and how slow of heart to believe all that the prophets have declared! Was it not necessary that the Messiah should suffer these things and then enter into his glory?" Then beginning with Moses and all the prophets, he interpreted to them the things about himself in all the scriptures. As they came near the village to which they were going, he walked ahead as if he were going on. But they urged him strongly, saying, "Stay with us, because it is almost evening and the day is now nearly over." So he went in to stay with them. When he was at the table with them, he took bread, blessed and broke it, and gave it to them. Then their eyes were opened, and they recognized him; and he vanished from their sight. They said to each other, "Were not our hearts burning within us while he was talking to us on the road, while he was opening the scriptures to us?" That same hour they got up and returned to Jerusalem; and they found the eleven and their companions gathered together. They were saying, "The Lord has risen indeed, and he has appeared to Simon!"

– Luke 24:13–21, 25–34

Bleib mit deiner Gnade / *Stay with us*

This story tells us how two men leave behind failure, anger, and sadness, and how they discover the source of peace, joy, and communion that nothing can destroy. This source is a person; to draw from it, to encounter it, we have to turn away from what obstructs the eyes of our souls.

We discover the two disciples as they are returning to their village defeated, leaving their companions behind. Caught up in their misfortunes, they do not recognize the one who joins them on the road. At the end of the story, forgetting their weariness, their doubts, and the dangers that threaten them, they run back to Jerusalem because they have something very important to tell those they had left. They are able to live for others once again.

The risen Christ comes to join the disciples where they are, entering into their rhythms, listening to their complaints and their incomprehension. He does not reproach them for running away and repudiating him. Nothing about his appearance is striking. All he does is repeat the gestures he performed so many times when he was with them, saying the words he said so often. But since he has lived out to the end what these words were pointing to, now they take on a whole new authority. The scriptures, which previously were pointing toward the future, have now come to fulfillment. The sharing of bread, which anticipated the gift of self, now expresses the fact that Jesus' entire being has become an offering.

What happened during those days in Jerusalem was not an accident. It was announced and prepared ahead of time, and that becomes a strong incentive to discern God's hope and to struggle to make it a reality. By giving his life to the end, Jesus opens a way so that, in our turn, we can give ourselves each day and so be creators of communion.

- In what circumstances have I discovered that I needed a source of forgiveness and peace?
- Have I ever had to remain alongside someone who was going through a difficult time? What helped me in this?

Jesus, light of our hearts, we would like never to abandon you by the wayside. And when we let you transfigure our weaknesses, unexpected resources appear within us.

Toward a Healing in the Depths

As Jesus and his disciples and a large crowd were leaving Jericho, Bartimaeus son of Timaeus, a blind beggar, was sitting by the roadside. When he heard that it was Jesus of Nazareth, he began to shout out and say, "Jesus, Son of David, have mercy on me!" Many sternly ordered him to be quiet, but he cried out even more loudly, "Son of David, have mercy on me!" Jesus stood still and said, "Call him here." And they called the blind man, saying to him, "Take heart; get up, he is calling you." So throwing off his cloak, he sprang up and came to Jesus. Then Jesus said to him, "What do you want me to do for you?" The blind man said to him, "My teacher, let me see again." Jesus said to him, "Go; your faith has made you well." Immediately he regained his sight and followed him on the way.

– Mark 10:46–52

Jesus, remember me

Bartimaeus, a blind man condemned to beg, is seen as a disturbance by those who are walking along with Jesus on the way to Jerusalem, the place where everything will be brought to fulfillment. But his cry overcomes all obstacles and reaches Christ. Jesus stops. He is not so absorbed by his goal that he no longer sees the suffering around him. Is it not, in fact, this suffering, before which humans flee, that he has come to take upon himself? In his eyes there are no outcasts.

What is striking in this story is that the healing takes place through a dialogue that reveals the astonishment, or even the admiration, of Jesus for this blind man. This rejected beggar has already rediscovered his human dignity. What trust there is in this cry: "Have mercy on me!" He runs toward Christ, even leaving behind his cloak in which he had collected money. And Jesus' question, "What do you want?", incites him to go to the very extremity of trusting. He does not ask for alms, but dares to say, "I want to see!" Healed, he then follows Jesus on his journey.

All of us are in need of healing. The cry of the blind man becomes our own cry in the *Kyrie eleison* of the liturgy, which seeks to replace the bitterness in us with trust. Our heart turns toward Christ, who suffers with us. And he gives us what is necessary to follow him on his road toward the Resurrection. Our trust awakens the admiration of Christ, and healing, a new freedom, begins in our depths.

- How does the attitude of Bartimaeus help me to renew my prayer?
- Do we sometimes become insensitive to people that we meet because we are too fixed on our own aims?

O Christ, you are united to every human being, even if they are unaware of it. Still more, risen from the dead, you come to heal the secret wound of the soul. And for each person the gates of a heartfelt compassion are opened.

"Come to Me, All You That Are Weary"

At that time Jesus said, "I thank you, Father, Lord of heaven and earth, because you have hidden these things from the wise and the intelligent and have revealed them to infants; yes, Father, for such was your gracious will. All things have been handed over to me by my Father; and no one knows the Son except the Father, and no one knows the Father except the Son and anyone to whom the Son chooses to reveal him. Come to me, all you that are weary and are carrying heavy burdens, and I will give you rest. Take my yoke upon you, and learn from me; for I am gentle and humble in heart, and you will find rest for your souls. For my yoke is easy, and my burden is light."

— Matthew 11:25–30

Beati voi poveri / *How blessed the poor in heart*

Jesus is faced with a big failure: he has been rejected in the cities where he began to announce God's Reign, and he expresses his suffering with harsh words (see vv. 20–24).

But then he returns to what has inspired him from the beginning of his public life, those words that God said to him, "This is my Son, the Beloved, with whom I am well pleased" (Matthew 3:17). Now there is no voice from heaven, as there was at his baptism, but only a simple reminder in prayer of God's words. And in this difficult situation, the words he heard at the beginning grow deeper in him, expressing the mystery of his entire being. Jesus does not receive any greater clarity about the future, but the situation is illuminated "vertically," so to speak.

Jesus can continue to announce God's presence, not like "the wise and the intelligent" but like someone who is "gentle and humble in heart," without imposing anything. And already his disciples are associated with him in proclaiming the Kingdom of God in this disarming way. And so praise springs up, for, in spite of the failure, his mystery is communicated, "revealed" to human beings.

The task that Christ gives us, in other words, the commandment to love God and our neighbor, is not an additional burden. To "learn from him" means hearing in our consciences, in our turn, that we are loved by God forever. In this way we enter into the same relationship that Jesus has with the Father. That is his "yoke," without which our earth cannot be plowed up nor bear fruit.

- • Are there words in the Bible that help me to go forward even in difficult situations?
- • Where do I see the Church reflecting particularly well the image of God who is kindness and who does not impose himself?
- • What difficult events have led me to deepen my image of God?

Savior of every life, in following you we choose to love and never to harden our hearts. And even were the depths of our being assailed by a trial, one way forward remains open—the way of serene trust.

Walk!

When he saw Peter and John about to go into the temple, a man lame from birth asked them for alms. Peter looked intently at him, as did John, and said, "Look at us." And he fixed his attention on them, expecting to receive something from them. But Peter said, "I have no silver or gold, but what I have I give you; in the name of Jesus Christ of Nazareth, stand up and walk."

– Acts 3:3–6

L'ajuda em vindrà (canon)

My help comes from the Lord, from the Lord our God who made heaven and earth.

Peter did not run away from facing the suffering of the man crippled from birth. He did not look for the "causes." He let himself be touched by the drama of that resigned person, who had only his handicap to awaken the pity of passers-by and to get from them enough to survive. In the eyes of all, that man presented the face of a fallen and absurd humanity that seemed to doom God's plan to failure.

Peter had no explanation for the mystery of that situation. But he could witness to and share what he himself had discovered: trust in Christ is stronger than anything else. Fears, acts of cowardice, and despair cannot destroy it. From the "Come, follow me!" that Peter heard by the lake until the "Do you love me?" after the Resurrection, Jesus had always shown him that trust is possible, because he himself was the first to run the risk of trusting.

"In the name of Jesus Christ..." Now Peter is filled with the Spirit of Christ and acts in his name. He proclaims both his communion with Christ and his hope for the handicapped man. Peter can expect something for someone who no longer expects anything. He can believe in the future of the one who was trapped in failure or suffering. The beggar was looking for something that would just enable him to survive. Peter dared to offer him a sharing in the secret of his life, so that God's glory would be manifested in him.

Putting Christ's call into practice means discovering in it a treasure that will never be lacking and with which we can respond to the expectations that we encounter. Sharing that call means living Christ for others.

- How am I already living out Christ's call?
- How can I dare to share that call with others?

God of mercy, when we are bewildered by the incomprehensible suffering of the innocent, come to enable us to manifest, by the lives that we live, a reflection of the compassion of Christ.

In the Light of the Resurrection

While he was blessing them, Jesus withdrew from them and was carried up into heaven.

– Luke 24:51

Per crucem (canon)

By your cross and passion, by your holy resurrection, set us free, O Lord.

Long before entering on the road that will lead him to the cross, Jesus begins preparing his companions for his coming death. After his resurrection, Christ takes up, as it were, from where he had left off: he "[opens] their minds to understand the scriptures," sends them out, and urges them to wait for the coming of the Holy Spirit. The departure at his ascension is thus emptied of sadness and passive resignation.

In our own lives, the departure of a loved one can become an occasion for meeting the risen Lord and for opening ourselves to our own resurrection. However, at the moment of departure itself, suffering exposes us to the risk of despair. Despair sows confusion and would have us believe that nothing remains outside of pain, absurdity, and misfortune. Such suffering is part of that passover, which is Easter, the birth into a new life.

Truth is not to be found in the emptiness we may wish to analyze or in explanations that would only serve to justify separation. The truth, indeed, is that there is no separation. And yet, it is the heart alone that can say it, and we must listen to its voice in silence. "Even though we once knew Christ from a human point of view, we know him no longer in that way" (2 Corinthians 5:16).

When Christ leaves, his place remains empty. And we must leave it free, without giving in to worry or impatience. Knowing that this same place is filled by his presence is the most precious of treasures one can "possess." It is there that the Spirit of the risen Christ awaits us. Neither separations, nor time, nor even forgetfulness can still the heart that has chosen to love.

- In what ways can I prepare myself and those entrusted to me to live out the separations that are part of life and to do so in the light of Christ?
- What helps to sustain us as we wait for the presence of the comforting Spirit, the one who comes to dwell within every human separation?

Jesus, risen Lord, you welcome into endless life those who have gone before us. They are already contemplating the invisible, and they sometimes remain so close to us. When there are times of suffering, it makes you love us even more. And by your Holy Spirit, you comfort, you bring peace.

Encountering the Risen Christ

Mary stood weeping outside the tomb. As she wept, she bent over to look into the tomb; and she saw two angels in white, sitting where the body of Jesus had been lying, one at the head and the other at the feet. They said to her, "Woman, why are you weeping?" She said to them, "They have taken away my Lord, and I do not know where they have laid him." When she had said this, she turned around and saw Jesus standing there, but she did not know that it was Jesus. Jesus said to her, "Woman, why are you weeping? Whom are you looking for?" Supposing him to be the gardener, she said to him, "Sir, if you have carried him away, tell me where you have laid him, and I will take him away." Jesus said to her, "Mary!" She turned and said to him in Hebrew, "Rabbouni!" (which means Teacher). Jesus said to her, "Do not hold on to me, because I have not yet ascended to the Father. But go to my brothers and say to them, 'I am ascending to my Father and your Father, to my God and your God.'" Mary Magdalene went and announced to the disciples, "I have seen the Lord"; and she told them that he had said these things to her.

– John 20:11–18

Christus resurrexit / *Jesus Christ is risen*

The encounter with the mystery of the Resurrection can be recognized first and foremost by the transformation it causes in those who are its witnesses. Mary of Magdala had been close to Jesus during his life on earth. Now left utterly disconsolate by his death, she attempts in vain to keep alive at least some fragments of that vanished relationship, memories symbolized for her by the tomb and the corpse.

Her attitude, in human terms worthy of commiseration, nonetheless keeps her from being fully present to the reality surrounding her. She notices neither the presence of heavenly messengers, harbingers of a new day, nor that of the risen Christ himself. It is only when Christ calls her by name that the spell is broken, and she experiences a new beginning: twice the passage uses the expression "turning round" (vv. 14, 16), a verb that in Hebrew is used for conversion of heart.

Overcome by joy, she still has a further step to take. The restored relationship will not be a mere copy of the previous one, before Jesus' death. Mary must give up all claims to "possession," all thought of having Jesus for her own, and set out in the wake of the Living One. It is only by going toward others, beginning with the community of disciples, that she can remain intimate with Christ. A relationship with the risen Lord turns disciples into living words who call others, in the name of God, to give up all forms of arrogance or despair in order to become part of a universal communion.

- What keeps me from perceiving what God is accomplishing in and around me?
- Have I known times when Christ called me by name? What enables us to distinguish his call from so many other invitations?
- To whom can I go in order to communicate an unexpected joy?

Jesus, our trust, ever since your resurrection, your light has been shining within us. And so we can still tell you: we love you without having seen you, though we still do not see you we believe, and you seek to shower upon us a joy beyond words, which already transfigures us.

REDISCOVERING HOPE

"Out of the Depths I Cry to You!"

Out of the depths I cry to you, O Lord.
Lord, hear my voice!
Let your ears be attentive
to the voice of my supplications!
If you, O Lord, should mark iniquities,
Lord, who could stand?
But there is forgiveness with you,
so that you may be revered.
I wait for the Lord, my soul waits,
and in his word I hope;
my soul waits for the Lord
more than those who watch for the morning,
more than those who watch for the morning.
O Israel, hope in the Lord!
For with the Lord there is steadfast love,
and with him is great power to redeem.
It is he who will redeem Israel
from all its iniquities.

— Psalm 130

El Senyor / *In the Lord*

76

This psalm is a cry of hope. How can this be possible? The psalmist seems to be in despair. But in saying: "I cry to you, Lord" (v. 1) and "Lord, hear my voice" (v. 2), he dares to lift up his song to God. Even in times of difficulty, he places his trust in God. The path that is closed becomes a path of hope.

But what is hope? By reading this psalm, we understand that hope is something better than human optimism. To hope is to live with an inner conviction that what we desire will come to pass, "more than those who watch for the morning" (v. 6), even if we cannot see this at present. As Saint Paul writes, "Hope that is seen is not hope. For who hopes for what is seen? But if we hope for what we do not see, we wait for it with patience" (Romans 8:24–25). The mystery is that often we learn this only when we are at the bottom of an abyss, when the only way to go forward is to trust.

Hope needs roots, a strong foundation. The psalmist's hope is based on God's love for him. He knows that this love is forgiveness: "with you is forgiveness" (v. 4). His hope is built on the experience of God's unconditional love.

Hope doesn't trap us, but, on the contrary, opens us. Hope is communicative. After having recalled the reasons for his hope, the psalmist says to the people, "O Israel, hope in the Lord" (v. 7a). He sees God's generosity overflowing: "With him is great power to redeem" (v. 7b).

- How does the image of watchers waiting for daybreak help me understand hope?
- What am I hoping for in my personal life, for my people, and for the Church?

Where is the source of hope and of joy for us? We find it in you, God of love, who never stops searching for us and finds in us the profound beauty of the human soul.

The One Who Awakens Hope

Many crowds followed Jesus, and he cured all of them, and he ordered them not to make him known. This was to fulfill what had been spoken through the prophet Isaiah: "Here is my servant, whom I have chosen, my beloved, with whom my soul is well pleased. I will put my Spirit upon him, and he will proclaim justice to the Gentiles. He will not wrangle or cry aloud, nor will anyone hear his voice in the streets. He will not break a bruised reed or quench a smoldering wick until he brings justice to victory. And in his name the Gentiles will hope."

— Matthew 12:15–21

Christe Salvator

Christ the Savior, Son of the Father, grant us peace.

Everywhere he went, Jesus knew how to awaken hope. Like no one else, he came up with the word or act that could bring people back to life. In this text, we see at first that he is followed closely by the crowd; he cannot get away from them. And the words in the passage help us understand that he is willing to help without a trace of hesitation: "and he cured all of them" (v. 15). But immediately he leads them further on: "He ordered them not to make him known" (v. 16). The evangelist, apparently astonished at Jesus' attitude, turns to a text from the Book of Isaiah. How can we understand the behavior of this man who brings others to life and who does not want to draw attention to himself?

The prophet describes a man upon whom the Spirit will rest and who will proclaim judgment, in other words, all the good that God asks for and helps to grow in us. But this servant achieves this without raising his voice (see v. 19) and with a gentleness that does not break even the reed about to fall. When the Gospel writer contemplates Christ, he sees someone sent from God who approaches a suffering person without breaking him or her, or who comes to someone on the edge of despair without extinguishing the weak light that remains. Christ never despises anyone. He sees what lies in the depths of every human being he meets. The person standing in front of Christ is never viewed merely as a means for him to propagate a message of some sort. That person is the one for whom Christ came, for whom he wants to give his life.

- In this passage, what challenges me the most? What do I see in Christ's attitude?
- Which people do I know who succeed in awakening hope around them? What is their "secret"? Can we see a reflection of Christ in them?

Jesus, our hope, your compassion is without limit. We are thirsting for your presence, you who tell us: "Why be afraid? Have no fear; I am here."

Finding in God a Meaning for Life

Now there was a Pharisee named Nicodemus, a leader of the Jews. He came to Jesus by night and said to him, "Rabbi, we know that you are a teacher who has come from God; for no one can do these signs that you do apart from the presence of God." Jesus answered him, "Very truly, I tell you, no one can see the kingdom of God without being born from above." Nicodemus said to him, "How can anyone be born after having grown old? Can one enter a second time into the mother's womb and be born?" Jesus answered, "Very truly, I tell you, no one can enter the kingdom of God without being born of water and Spirit. What is born of the flesh is flesh, and what is born of the Spirit is spirit. Do not be astonished that I said to you, 'You must be born from above.' The wind blows where it chooses, and you hear the sound of it, but you do not know where it comes from or where it goes. So it is with everyone who is born of the Spirit." Nicodemus said to him, "How can these things be?" Jesus answered him, "Are you a teacher of Israel, and yet you do not understand these things? Very truly, I tell you, we speak of what we know and testify to what we have seen; yet you do not receive our testimony. If I have told you about earthly things and you do not believe, how can you believe if I tell you about heavenly things? No one has ascended into heaven except the one who descended from heaven, the Son of Man. And just as Moses lifted up the serpent in the wilderness, so must the Son of Man be lifted up, that whoever believes in him may have eternal life. For God so loved the world that he gave his only Son, so that everyone who believes in him may not perish but may have eternal life. Indeed, God did not send the Son into the world to condemn the world, but in order that the world might be saved through him."

– John 3:1–17

Tu sei sorgente viva

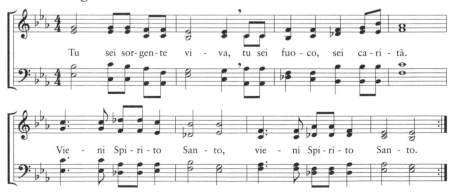

You are the living spring; you are fire and love. Come, Holy Spirit.

Birth is the moment in which one's life appears as both gift and call. I can be brought into the world only by the act of another person, by someone who is expecting me.

"Being born of the flesh" means being separated from one's mother's body and to become autonomous. It means taking on a face of one's own and becoming able to meet others face to face. Yet human life is not this alone. A person only becomes fully alive when he or she discovers, beyond themselves, a "why" or a "whom" to live for. If there is nothing to live for or if one is alone, a person will find neither the energy nor the motivation needed to set out on the road of life, with the suffering that entails.

"Being born from above" means discovering that our deepest identity is to be found ahead of us, in a process of becoming, where choices and responsibilities come into play. Recognizing clearly the "why" of our existence and anchoring it within God gives our desire a direction over the course of an entire lifetime.

"Being born of water" is a reference to a reality already evoked at Jesus' own baptism (see Matthew 3:16–17). Coming up out of the dark waters together with Christ means being liberated from the power of evil, from fear and death, in order to take part in his resurrection here and now.

To be born into this world by the Spirit who "makes us cry out Abba! Father!" (Romans 8:15) means leaving self-preoccupation behind and opening ourselves to God's hope for us, entering thereby into a life of communion. It means hearing, in silence and peace, the call of Christ who tells us of God's plan for us and draws us out of isolation.

- Which persons have brought me to birth in trust in God?
- How does the Father's gaze upon me help me to awaken others to the life of the Spirit?

Searching for you, Christ, means discovering your presence even in the lonely places deep within us. Happy those who surrender themselves to you. Happy those who approach you with trusting hearts.

"Why Are You Afraid?"

When evening had come, Jesus said to his disciples, "Let us go across to the other side." And leaving the crowd behind, they took him with them in the boat, just as he was. Other boats were with him. A great windstorm arose, and the waves beat into the boat, so that the boat was already being swamped. But he was in the stern, asleep on the cushion; and they woke him up and said to him, "Teacher, do you not care that we are perishing?" He woke up and rebuked the wind, and said to the sea, "Peace! Be still!" Then the wind ceased, and there was a dead calm. He said to them, "Why are you afraid? Have you still no faith?" And they were filled with great awe and said to one another, "Who then is this, that even the wind and the sea obey him?"

– Mark 4:35–41

Fiez-vous en Lui

Fi-ez-vous en Lui, ne craig-nez pas. La paix de Dieu gar-de-ra vos cœurs. Fi-ez-vous en Lui. Al-le-lu - ia, al-le-lu - ia!

Trust in Him and do not fear. God's peace will protect your hearts. Alleluia, alleluia!

In the evening, Jesus wanted to leave the place where he had been teaching for a long time. His disciples "took him in the boat just as he was"; the departure seemed rushed. Did Jesus feel threatened? He knew that the followers of Herod Antipas, the ruler of Galilee, were looking for a way to get rid of him (see Mark 3:6). Crossing to the other side, to "the country of the Gerasenes," Jesus and his disciples would be out of the reach of Herod's power.

But scarcely had they escaped danger from other human beings than the forces of nature attacked the little fishing boat belonging to the followers of Jesus. Even those experienced fishermen did not know what to do. They no longer recognized their Sea of Galilee: the waves were like the open jaws of the great Abyss, ready to swallow them forever. So they cried out with fear. And their distress was mingled with a reproach: "Do you not care that we are perishing?"

Then Jesus woke up. He had absolutely no part in the agitation surrounding him. He spoke two words, and everything quieted down. But how could he have fallen asleep on the cushion in the stern during a storm? Only a child could have done this. Jesus was not a child, but, as the psalm says, "he keeps his soul calmed and quieted, like a weaned child with its mother" (Psalms 131). The words to calm the storm arose from his silence in God. Centuries later, Isaac of Nineveh would say, "Quiet yourself, and heaven and earth will fill you with peace."

By asking "Have you still no faith?" Jesus showed that he did what he did for the sake of our faith. The one whom "wind and sea obey" also says to the cares, the fears, and the suffering that cause turmoil in our souls, "Peace! Be still!" Faith is nourished by the quiet created by the words spoken by Christ.

- How do I react in situations when my experience is not enough to allow me to find a way out?
- For the disciples, Jesus' words transformed a threatening reality, the stormy sea, into a place where a new encounter with him in peace became possible. What enables us today to find the quiet necessary for an act of trust?

Risen Jesus, mystery of a presence, you never want us to be tormented; you clothe us in your peace. And a Gospel joy comes to touch the depths of our souls.

"Arise! Let Your Soul Live!"

At the pool of Bethzatha, one man was there who had been ill for thirty-eight years. When Jesus saw him lying there and knew that he had been there a long time, he said to him, "Do you want to be made well?" The sick man answered him, "Sir, I have no one to put me into the pool when the water is stirred up; and while I am making my way, someone else steps down ahead of me." Jesus said to him, "Stand up, take your mat and walk." At once the man was made well, and he took up his mat and began to walk. Now that day was a sabbath. So the Jews said to the man who had been cured, "It is the sabbath; it is not lawful for you to carry your mat." But he answered them, "The man who made me well said to me, 'Take up your mat and walk.'" They asked him, "Who is the man who said to you, 'Take it up and walk'?" Now the man who had been healed did not know who it was, for Jesus had disappeared in the crowd that was there. Later Jesus found him in the temple and said to him, "See, you have been made well! Do not sin any more, so that nothing worse happens to you." The man went away and told the Jews that it was Jesus who had made him well. Therefore the Jews started persecuting Jesus, because he was doing such things on the sabbath. But Jesus answered them, "My Father is still working, and I also am working." For this reason the Jews were seeking all the more to kill him, because he was not only breaking the sabbath, but was also calling God his own Father, thereby making himself equal to God. Jesus said to them, "Very truly, I tell you, the Son can do nothing on his own, but only what he sees the Father doing; for whatever the Father does, the Son does likewise... Very truly, I tell you, anyone who hears my word and believes him who sent me, has eternal life, and does not come under judgment, but has passed from death to life."

– John 5:5–19, 24

Bonum est confidere

Bo- num est con - fi - de - re in Do - mi - no, bo- num spe - ra - re in Do - mi - no.

It is good to trust and hope in the Lord.

Jesus heals a sick man on the Sabbath day, a day when everyone is invited to look at the world with God's eyes. On the eve of the first Sabbath, God saw that all he had done was very good (see Genesis 1:31). Jesus also sees what is not yet good. He is attentive to the suffering of that crowd of sick people clustered around a pool, unable to enter the Temple nearby to take part in the celebrations there.

Jesus asks one of them, "Do you want to be healed?" The sick man hesitates, not daring to hope. He never had any luck. No one has ever helped him. He can walk a bit, but so slowly that he always gets there late. Jesus says to him, "Get up, take your mat and walk." The sick man trusts those words. He gets up and goes to the Temple. There, a little while later, Jesus speaks to him again, saying, "Sin no more." Before that, others had also warned the man not to sin because, by carrying his mat, he was not keeping the Sabbath commandment. But Jesus is speaking about sin in a deeper sense. The heart of sin does not consist in breaking a rule, for instance by working on the Sabbath day. "To sin" means literally "to miss the mark." In his discouragement, the sick man missed that for which human beings are made: to love life and to praise God. The thirty-eight years he spent lying there without doing anything echo the thirty-eight years during which Israel wandered in the wilderness far from the land of its happiness (see Deuteronomy 2:14).

This healing is a "sign," the visible tip of an infinitely more immense reality. It manifests God's work. God is always active. Each day, at every moment, God gives life, saves life from absurdity, gives it a meaning. We do not see Christ, but we have his words in the Gospel. In hearing him tell us "Get up!" we "cross over from death to life."

- Why did the sick man not really dare to answer Jesus' question: "Do you want to be healed?" What made him prudent, or even hesitant?
- Do I dare tell Christ what I would like for my life? Does what would make me "get up" and seem to be possible, or inaccessible?
- What do the words of Christ, "Get up and walk!", mean for me today?

God of all loving, we long to hear your call resound in us: "Arise, let your soul live!" We never wish to choose darkness or discouragement, but to welcome the radiance of praise.

85

Hoping against All Hope

The word of the Lord came to Elijah, saying, "Go now to Zarephath, which belongs to Sidon, and live there; for I have commanded a widow there to feed you." So he set out and went to Zarephath. When he came to the gate of the town, a widow was there gathering sticks; he called to her and said, "Bring me a little water in a vessel, so that I may drink." As she was going to bring it, he called to her and said, "Bring me a morsel of bread in your hand." But she said, "As the Lord your God lives, I have nothing baked, only a handful of meal in a jar, and a little oil in a jug; I am now gathering a couple of sticks, so that I may go home and prepare it for myself and my son, that we may eat it, and die." Elijah said to her, "Do not be afraid; go and do as you have said; but first make me a little cake of it and bring it to me, and afterwards make something for yourself and your son. For thus says the Lord the God of Israel: The jar of meal will not be emptied and the jug of oil will not fail until the day that the Lord sends rain on the earth." She went and did as Elijah said, so that she as well as he and her household ate for many days. The jar of meal was not emptied, neither did the jug of oil fail, according to the word of the Lord that he spoke by Elijah.

– 1 Kings 17:8–16

Notre âme attend / Our soul is waiting

Notre âme at-tend le Sei-gneur. En lui la joie de no-tre cœur.
Our soul is wait-ing for God. Our hearts find joy in the Lord.

During a period of severe drought, Elijah hears God's call to set out. At first he withdraws to a solitary place located near a stream, far from any settlement. Turning northward, he then heads to a foreign land by the name of Sidon (which corresponds roughly to present-day Lebanon). The experience of the Israelites of long ago who had lived in Egypt and then crossed the desert becomes, in a sense, his own.

Once in Sidon, he comes to the town of Zarephath. As any tired traveller might do, he calls out to a passerby and asks for some water to drink. Upon seeing that she seems well disposed to grant his request, he asks for a piece of bread as well. But that turns out to be too much for her. She pours out her despair; she is a widow, alone and poor, without even enough to feed her child. With the wood she is collecting, she intends to bake a last cake with the handful of flour she has left, after which she expects they will die.

At that point, Elijah asks her for more than a little water and bread. He asks her to trust in God. God will provide what is needed to live, even if she is a foreigner and does not know the God of Israel. The God to which Elijah bears witness looks after all who hope in him. She then expresses her trust by offering her guest the little that she possesses.

"Hold fast to love and justice, and wait continually for your God" (Hosea 12:6). Without knowing it, the widow of Zarephath puts into practice these words, which express in a very simple manner the covenant God has made with his people. Through her deeds and her hospitality, she does what she felt was her duty as a human being. Her trust in God, when she is faced with a future with no prospects, preserves her from discouragement.

- What touches me in the attitude of the widow of Zarephath?
- What aspects of our own future may make us worry?
- In what ways, however limited, can we share with others and offer them hospitality in the present so as not to remain passive?

God of mercy, enable us to surrender ourselves to you in silence and in love. Such trust does not come easily to our human condition. But you open within us the way that leads toward the radiance of a hope.

Keeping Alert, Discerning, and Praying

Now after John was arrested, Jesus came to Galilee, proclaiming the good news of God, and saying, "The time is fulfilled, and the kingdom of God has come near; repent, and believe in the good news."

– Mark 1:14–15

Venite, exultemus Domino / *O come and let us sing to God*

"The kingdom of God has come near!" Jesus' message is summed up in those words. Isaiah had announced its future coming, but Jesus says, more radically, "It is already here!" When he speaks these words, the times are not good: John the Baptist has just been thrown into prison. There is a lack of hope, politically as well as spiritually. In a world where violence and the law of the jungle seem to win out, where even with the best of intentions life together seems inconceivable, Jesus wants to make people attentive to a new way forward: God is here! God's kingdom is hidden in the world like yeast in the flour (see Matthew 13:33). We can pray to "our Father who is in secret" (Matthew 6:6).

Christ is turned toward God from the beginning (see John 1:1). And he wants to lead us along that road. Far from being a flight from the world, this road allows us to be much more present to the world, to people's joys as well as their sufferings. Living a life turned toward God involves a twofold activity: Jesus shows goodness himself, by healing and forgiving, but he also brings to light signs of God's presence that he discovers in others, like the widow who gives all she has (see Mark 12:44) or the Roman centurion who shows such trust that Jesus admires him (see Luke 7:9), or the disciples who leave everything to follow him.

What is astonishing is Jesus' simplicity. And he invites us to have the same simplicity: "keeping alert" (Mark 13:37), "believing" in the presence of God's love for everyone, rooting our lives with perseverance in this love and discovering signs of it, especially in acts of charity and beauty. Through humble events, God speaks to everyone with infinite discretion. It is up to us to discern God's presence, discovering day by day in the events of our life a word from God.

And then we discover that we are supported. The Holy Spirit that was with Jesus throughout his life (Luke 1:35; 3:22; 4:14; 24:49) "makes us cross over to the newness of Christ" (Irenaeus of Lyons). A new vitality, a living hope, animates our life, when we dare to see God at work even in difficult situations, creating life and communion.

- What signs of the presence of God's reign are supports for me in my life today?

Holy Spirit, poured out in every human being, you give freedom and spontaneity. You give the zest for life to those who are losing it. You come to deliver us from discouragement.

89

Living in the Present Moment

Thus says the Lord,
who makes a way in the sea,
a path in the mighty waters,
who brings out chariot and horse,
army and warrior;
they lie down, they cannot rise,
they are extinguished, quenched like a wick:
Do not remember the former things,
or consider the things of old.
I am about to do a new thing;
now it springs forth, do you not perceive it?
I will make a way in the wilderness
and rivers in the desert.
The wild animals will honor me,
the jackals and the ostriches;
for I give water in the wilderness,
rivers in the desert,
to give drink to my chosen people,
the people whom I formed for myself
so that they might declare my praise.

  – Isaiah 43:16–21

Wait for the Lord

At the heart of the people of Israel's faith is the account of the exodus from Egypt: God liberates the former slaves from the yoke of bondage and brings them safely across the sea. In celebrating the defeat of the Egyptians, the story, in fact, wishes to emphasize how powerless the forces of evil are to thwart God's loving designs.

And now, centuries later, an anonymous prophet in the land of exile seems to be encouraging his hearers to forget this great act of God! Is he attempting to subvert the religion of his contemporaries at the very moment when they are in such dire straits?

What the prophet is combating, rather, is the escape into nostalgia. Two attitudes are possible with regard to past events. We can use them to deplore the present, in a vain attempt to turn back the clock. Or else we can remember that the same God who saved those who went before us is still with us, ready and able to accomplish a similar wonder today. In this way, reflecting on the past becomes a springboard to deal with the present and to believe in the future.

For this prophet, God is above all a permanent source of newness. By looking at what God did in the past, we become capable of discerning how he is at work here and now. We draw the courage and the hope to live fully in the present moment, convinced that the best is yet to come.

- When have I been tempted to view the past nostalgically?
- How can I use the past to find courage for the present and hope for the future?
- What changes in my life when I realize that God always creates something new?

God of all mercy, you bury our past in the heart of Christ, and you are going to take care of our future.

Being Drawn into God's Love

Sing aloud, O daughter Zion;
shout, O Israel!
Rejoice and exult with all your heart,
O daughter Jerusalem!
The Lord has taken away the judgments against you,
he has turned away your enemies.
The king of Israel, the Lord, is in your midst;
you shall fear disaster no more.
On that day it shall be said to Jerusalem:
Do not fear, O Zion;
do not let your hands grow weak.
The Lord, your God, is in your midst,
a warrior who gives victory;
he will rejoice over you with gladness,
he will renew you in his love;
he will exult over you with loud singing.
– Zephaniah 3:14–17

Sanctum nomen Domini

My soul magnifies the holy name of the Lord.

Toward the end of the ministry of the prophet Zephaniah, there is no longer any king or Temple in Jerusalem. The joyful celebrations and the pilgrimages are only a distant memory. If people still think about them, it is with sadness and regret. War, famine, and exile have almost wiped out God's people. Very little is left of its former glory. But now, for this "remnant of Israel," the prophet has an astonishing message: "Rejoice!" "Shout for joy!" "Exult with all your heart!" He cannot find enough words to proclaim to them the message of happiness.

Fear is a great obstacle to joy—fear of the tragic consequences of the errors of the past, agonizing worry about the future. To open a space where joy can develop, the Lord combats the causes of fear. He "has turned your enemy away." He "has taken away the judgments against you," making sure that your faults do not lead to misfortune. His forgiveness reactivates "weak hands." It is true that Jerusalem no longer has a king, no organized life. Everything must begin anew. But why be discouraged if God himself comes as "king of Israel," the one who takes care of his people?

It is as if Zephaniah saw the Lord coming. God comes like a young man in love, singing and dancing. "He rejoices with gladness," "He exults over you with loud singing." God lets his people glimpse that in the depths of his being he is joy. "The Lord rejoices in his works" (Psalms 104:31). His love is joyful, and for that reason it is always new, always surprising. "The Kingdom of God," says the apostle Paul, "is joy in the Holy Spirit" (Romans 14:17). The Holy Spirit brings together two joys—God's joy and our joy. One calls out to the other; one leads the other as in a dance, in the festival where God and human beings are united.

- How can we leave some room for the spirit of celebration in our daily lives?
- Where, at what moment, on what occasions, can I feel joy being reborn in me?
- What obstacles to joy would I like God to remove?

Jesus, our joy, you want us to have hearts that are simple, a kind of springtime of the heart. And then the complications of existence do not paralyze us so much. You tell us: "Don't worry; I am with you always."

"May My Joy Be in You!"

Jesus said to his disciples, "I have said these things to you so that my joy may be in you, and that your joy may be complete. This is my commandment, that you love one another as I have loved you. No one has greater love than this, to lay down one's life for one's friends."

– John 15:11–13

Laudate omnes gentes / *Sing praises, all you peoples*

Lau - da - te om - nes gen - tes, lau - da - te Do - mi - num. Lau - da - te om - nes gen - tes, lau - da - te Do - mi - num. Lau -

Sing prais - es, all you peo - ples, sing prais - es to the Lord. Sing prais - es, all you peo - ples, sing prais - es to the Lord. Sing

94

Jesus says these words at the end of his time together with his disciples, on the eve of his passion. When he is about to face public humiliation, official condemnation, the desertion of his disciples, and suffering, then, when violence and fear might seem to overwhelm everything, Jesus experiences joy.

He does not want to communicate knowledge or instructions, but to ensure that his own joy will continually spring up afresh in his friends. His whole effort is directed to uncovering that wellspring deep within them, so that the approaching tempest will not be able to destroy their joy. His joy is not the "satisfaction" of someone who has made it, but rather the foundation of his life, his deepest motivation from the start of his mission. "All my joy (favor) is in you" are words that Jesus hears at his baptism. To be his Father's happiness in the midst of human beings is what has sustained his mission.

By solemnly bequeathing his "commandment" to his friends, Jesus lends all his authority to his words. They distill the very meaning of his existence. Jesus turns his disciples into leaders and bearers of these words, sent out toward the future. He places in them a wellspring where the vitality of their lives will be renewed. By giving what lies at the source of his own commitment, Jesus makes it possible for them to give everything. To give their lives, day by day, letting Jesus' life grow within them.

- How can we remain close to the wellspring of Christ's joy? For whom can we live in happiness and bear witness to joy?
- How can I give my life at every moment—when my life is so imperfect and I don't always see things clearly?

Jesus, our trust, your Gospel brings with it such a fine hope that we would like to give ourselves to the very end in order to follow you. And irresistibly the question arises: where is the source of such hope? It lies in surrendering ourselves to you, Christ.

GOING FORWARD WITH DISCERNMENT

An Open and Willing Heart

At Gibeon the Lord appeared to Solomon in a dream by night; and God said, "Ask what I should give you." And Solomon said, "You have shown great and steadfast love to your servant my father David, because he walked before you in faithfulness, in righteousness, and in uprightness of heart toward you; and you have kept for him this great and steadfast love, and have given him a son to sit on his throne today. And now, O Lord my God, you have made your servant king in place of my father David, although I am only a little child; I do not know how to go out or come in. And your servant is in the midst of the people whom you have chosen, a great people, so numerous they cannot be numbered or counted. Give your servant therefore an understanding mind to govern your people, able to discern between good and evil; for who can govern this your great people?" It pleased the Lord that Solomon had asked this. God said to him, "Because you have asked this, and have not asked for yourself long life or riches, or for the life of your enemies, but have asked for yourself understanding to discern what is right, I now do according to your word. Indeed I give you a wise and discerning mind; no one like you has been before you and no one like you shall arise after you. I give you also what you have not asked, both riches and honor all your life; no other king shall compare with you. If you will walk in my ways, keeping my statutes and my commandments, as your father David walked, then I will lengthen your life."

– 1 Kings 3:5–14

Lumière de nos cœurs / *O light of every heart*

Lu - miè - re de nos cœurs, Sei - gneur, che - min d'é - ter - ni - té,
O light of ev - 'ry heart, O way of all e - ter - ni - ty,

ô vie pour tou - te la ter - re dans ton Es - prit ras - sem - ble - nous.
O life, true source of all liv - ing, your Spir - it, Lord, is gath - er - ing us.

Al - lé - lu - ia! A - mour de tout a - mour,
Al - le - lu - ia! O love of ev - 'ry love,

Sei - gneur, tu nous ap - pel - les. Ta voix dé - chi - re nos nuits
O Lord, we hear you call - ing, your voice breaks in - to our night

et s'ouvrent en nous les por - tes de lou - an - ge. Al - lé - lu - ia!
and in our hearts the gates of praise o - pen. Al - le - lu - ia!

In a dream, the Lord offered the young king Solomon the gift of his choice. Aware of his lack of experience and his limits, the king asked for "an understanding mind (heart) to govern [God's] people, able to discern between good and evil." God then made him understand that in asking for wisdom, he had found the key that would unlock all the other doors as well.

In the ancient civilizations of the Middle East, wisdom was, first of all, practical intelligence, the "common sense" necessary to succeed in life. But very quickly in the Bible it took on a religious meaning: a wise person is one who walks along the ways of God, who is able to discern what God wants and put it into practice. And this wisdom, which is the subjective side of God's plan, can only come from God himself; it is a gift. When they try to achieve it by their own cleverness alone, human beings go astray in the illusions of a false autonomy and a magical omnipotence that in the final analysis leave them empty.

It is not by chance that at the same time, a sage was setting down in writing a story in which a woman and a man, instead of listening to God's voice, stole the fruit of "the tree of the knowledge of good and evil" (see Genesis 3). The basic choice offered to human beings is always the same: either to center everything on themselves, or on God; to attempt to be their own source, or to welcome everything as a gift. In the language of the Bible, "the fear of the Lord is the beginning of wisdom," in other words, an attitude of respect before the unfathomable Mystery at the heart of life (see Proverbs 9:10). Solomon understood that he was only a servant of the God of great generosity, who wants to bestow everything on human beings. The king's limits were, therefore, no longer an obstacle to the fulfillment of God's plan, since when God encounters a heart that is open and willing, he can use what seems worthless to lead us toward the fullness of life.

- What aspects of the contemporary world make us forget that life and wisdom are gifts to be welcomed? How can we bear witness in this context to a God who is a source of generosity?
- What indications can I find in this story for dealing with situations when I become aware of my limits?

God of all eternity, whether we know it or not, your Holy Spirit is light within us. That light illuminates the dark shadows of our souls, suffusing them with an invisible presence.

An Ongoing Creation

So when they had come together, they asked him, "Lord, is this the time when you will restore the kingdom to Israel?" He replied, "It is not for you to know the times or periods that the Father has set by his own authority. But you will receive power when the Holy Spirit has come upon you; and you will be my witnesses in Jerusalem, in all Judea and Samaria, and to the ends of the earth."

– Acts 1:6–8

In manus tuas, Pater

Into your hands, Father, I commend my spirit.

How can we know God's will? When Jesus, risen from the dead, gathers his disciples once again, they think that now they are well placed to discover the great plan God has conceived for his people, and, indeed, for all the inhabitants of earth. The question they ask him, using expressions current at that time and place, attempts to discover something that human beings have always wanted to know in order to live authentically.

The first answer Jesus gives seems disappointing. He tells them that this knowledge is reserved to the Father alone. It is not that he does not want to share it with us. But "to know the times or periods" from without, we would have to be God. Human beings exist within time and, therefore, cannot distance themselves from the events of their history. Otherwise, they would no longer be what in fact they are.

Nevertheless, Jesus ultimately does give a positive answer to their question. You will receive the power of the Spirit, he tells them, and this will enable you to bear witness to me. Although no knowledge of God's plan is possible from the outside, that plan will be revealed to them from within; they will discover it by living it! The gift of the Spirit sets the disciples of Christ on the road of witnessing. They will continue the work of their teacher by undertaking a pilgrimage of trust across the earth. The Spirit, who sheds light on this road step by step, will never leave them. This good news remains difficult for the part of ourselves that wants to know everything ahead of time before making a commitment, but in the final analysis it is the only way our freedom can come fully into its own. It brings us into contact with the God who imposes nothing, whose will is not a trap, the God who offers us the possibility of a permanent creation with him.

- What helps me to discern the next step that the Spirit of God suggests to me in order to live out my faith in Christ?
- What allows me to trust in a God who does not reveal his plans ahead of time?

Jesus, our peace, you never abandon us. And the Holy Spirit always opens a way forward, the way that consists in resting in God, fathomless depth of compassion.

Called to Freedom

You were called to freedom, brothers and sisters; only do not use your freedom as an opportunity for self-indulgence, but through love become slaves to one another. For the whole law is summed up in a single commandment, "You shall love your neighbor as yourself." If, however, you bite and devour one another, take care that you are not consumed by one another. Live by the Spirit, I say... The fruit of the Spirit is love, joy, peace, patience, kindness, generosity, faithfulness, gentleness, and self-control. There is no law against such things.

– Galatians 5:13–16a, 22–23

Vieni Spirito creatore (canon) / *Come and pray in us*

At the heart of the Gospel is found freedom. The presence of the Holy Spirit liberates human beings from all kinds of determinisms to make them people who find their identities in their relationship with God alone (see Galatians 1:10). In his letter to the Galatians, Saint Paul is writing to people who confuse the liberty of the Spirit with a life with no reference points, and he tries to deepen their understanding of this fundamental reality.

The Spirit is the source of freedom, the apostle tells them, but freedom has nothing automatic about it. We need to make a choice, to live according to this Spirit in us. In Paul's language, we must "walk according to the Spirit." Otherwise, we fall prey to what Paul calls a "life according to the flesh." This obscure expression stands for a life without reference to God, closed to the help of God's vivifying and unifying love. Such a life can lead only to division and dispersion.

In fact, freedom is never found in a pure state. Every way of life has its consequences. To the "works of the flesh," Paul contrasts "the fruit of the Spirit," a single, many-sided reality: love, peace, goodness, trust, and so on. That is where true freedom is found, for such a life is creative; it does not lead to sterile isolation but engenders and unites. To enter it, there is one road: crossing over with Christ from death to life, consenting to the impulses of his Spirit at work in us.

- How can we live according to the Spirit in the concrete circumstances of our lives?
- How can we serve others through love?
- In what way is the Gospel a source of freedom for me?

Holy Spirit, we would like to welcome you with great simplicity. And it is above all through the heart that you enable us to penetrate the mystery of your invisible presence at the center of our souls.

The Risk of Trusting

As he walked by the Sea of Galilee, Jesus saw two brothers, Simon, who is called Peter, and Andrew his brother, casting a net into the sea—for they were fishermen. And he said to them, "Follow me, and I will make you fish for people." Immediately they left their nets and followed him.

– Matthew 4:18–20

Christe, lux mundi

Chri - ste, lux mun - di, qui se-qui-tur te ha - be-bit lu-men vi - tae, lu-men vi - tae.

O Christ, light of the world, whoever follows you will have the light of life.

"Come, follow me…" The fishermen from Galilee could have paid no attention to these words of a passing stranger. Since they took them seriously, however, their whole lives were changed. That was because they opened the depths of their beings to the call, and in that discreet invitation all of Jesus was already present: he was the one risking his expectations and his trust. Because trust in the Father was the whole of his life, he could dare to invite others to share his commitment. He opens a way of freedom, where the other is recognized as unique and irreplaceable. His boldness awakens the longing for a full life and a taste for risk.

Welcoming Christ's love means letting oneself be unsettled, hearing that invitation. We hear it in the silence of our hearts, when we open ourselves to God in prayer, giving God time and space, hearing it in those around us, even the lowliest. Through them, Christ invites us again and again without ever imposing himself. "Will you, once again, put trust at the beginning of everything?" he asks. "Can you accept that I, Christ, wish to make your life full through those I entrust to you?" Am I going to welcome this invitation, or am I going to withdraw, keeping my distance, free in theory but in fact isolated and accomplishing nothing? Taking Christ's invitation seriously also means preparing myself to take on other responsibilities: "I will make you fishers of people."

- How can I take seriously the freedom given to me?
- What risks can I take to build trust with others?

You, Christ, open our eyes to the wonder of your compassion. And we welcome your call as you say to us: "Come, follow me; in me you will find rest."

A Look of Goodness

Jesus said, "Your eye is the lamp of your body. If your eye is healthy, your whole body is full of light; but if it is not healthy, your body is full of darkness. Therefore consider whether the light in you is not darkness. If then your whole body is full of light, with no part of it in darkness, it will be as full of light as when a lamp gives you light with its rays."

– Luke 11:34–36

C'est toi ma lampe, Seigneur / *Your word, O Lord, is a light*

According to theories of vision in ancient times, the eye does not only capture light; it gives forth light as well. That is why Jesus could say, "Your eye is the lamp of the body." The eye is literally a lamp that illuminates. That is how they explained why some animals could see in the dark. A healthy eye gives off light. For a diseased eye, everything is darkness and confusion. In the words of Jesus, a healthy eye is literally a "simple" eye: a way of looking that is generous and straightforward. A diseased eye is a "bad" eye, blinded by jealousy or hatred. A Jewish writing that Jesus may have been familiar with said, "A good man does not have a dark eye, for he has compassion for everyone, even sinners."

Jesus' words, "If your eye is healthy, your whole body is full of light; but if it is not healthy, your body is full of darkness," can mean that the quality of our lives depends on the way we look at things. If you look around with simplicity and goodness, you will be in the light, and you will find your way. If you let jealousy blind you, in the end you will stumble in your own night.

Another translation is possible: "When your eye is healthy, [that shows that] your whole body is in the light, but when it is bad, [that means] your body is in darkness." This second interpretation fits better with the theory that the eye emits a subtle fire that is in the body. The following words confirm this: "Consider whether the light in you is not darkness." What matters is the light within. If you have night within you, your gaze will be hard and create difficulties. But when your inner life is illuminated and oriented toward love, a look of kindness sheds light around you, even if you are unaware of it.

- Why is our way of looking sometimes troubled and even dark?
- What can heal it, making it more transparent and open?
- What situations around us would need the light of a look of kindness?

Jesus, our joy, when we pray in silence, without words, the simple desire for your presence is already the beginning of faith. And in our life living water gushes forth: the goodness, and the selflessness that come from the Holy Spirit.

"Keep Your Heart with All Vigilance"

The path of the righteous is like the light of dawn,
which shines brighter and brighter until full day.
The way of the wicked is like deep darkness;
they do not know what they stumble over.
My child, be attentive to my words;
incline your ear to my sayings.
Do not let them escape from your sight;
keep them within your heart.
For they are life to those who find them,
and healing to all their flesh.
Keep your heart with all vigilance,
for from it flow the springs of life.
Put away from you crooked speech,
and put devious talk far from you.
Let your eyes look directly forward,
and your gaze be straight before you.
Keep straight the path of your feet,
and all your ways will be sure.
Do not swerve to the right or to the left;
turn your foot away from evil.

– Proverbs 4:18–27

Spiritus Jesu Christi

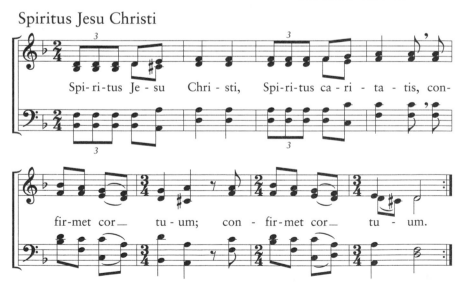

Spi-ri-tus Je-su Chri-sti, Spi-ri-tus ca-ri - ta - tis, con-
fir-met cor___ tu-um; con - fir-met cor___ tu - um.

May the Spirit of Christ Jesus, the Spirit of love, confirm you heart.

There is both a "path of the righteous" and a "way of the wicked," and we have to choose. Choosing integrity is not a guarantee that we will succeed. But those who turn neither to right nor to left root their lives in a promise. Their life has a direction; it is like "the light of dawn which shines brighter and brighter till full day." On the other road things become narrower and narrower, and people can come to a dead end without even realizing it.

We need to be particularly attentive to the way we speak to and look at others. "Put away from you crooked speech"; speak the truth and keep your promises. Trust can only grow if we can have confidence in what people say. Lies, half-truths, and deceitful words create a climate of mistrust and make people suspicious. "Let your gaze be straight before you." A transparent and generous way of seeing illuminates what it looks upon. It changes life around us, making it more peaceful and beautiful. But those whose eyes are masked by jealousy and made shifty by envy trap themselves and others in the darkness and confusion of their own hearts.

"Keep your heart with all vigilance." Here the heart stands for the deepest core of the person, his or her inner life, where everything comes into being before it emerges in words or acts. But the heart is above all the place of "the springs of life," where the Holy Spirit has hidden unsuspected resources. We do not create the wellspring, but we can make sure that nothing keeps it from flowing freely. "A good person," says Jesus, "out of the good treasure of the heart produces good" (Luke 6:45). Keeping watch over our inner lives as over a precious treasure, we will always have at our disposal a store of all kinds of good things.

- What helps us to make the choices we need to make each day?
- What kind of behavior enables us to foster trust? What attitudes are in danger of creating a climate of suspicion?
- How can I keep watch over my heart? How can I be attentive to the wellsprings the Holy Spirit causes to flow from it?

Holy Spirit, do not let our hearts be troubled, reassure us in our night, grant us your joy.

From Doubt to Trust

Thomas (who was called the Twin), one of the twelve, was not with them when Jesus came. So the other disciples told him, "We have seen the Lord." But he said to them, "Unless I see the mark of the nails in his hands, and put my finger in the mark of the nails and my hand in his side, I will not believe." A week later his disciples were again in the house, and Thomas was with them. Although the doors were shut, Jesus came and stood among them and said, "Peace be with you." Then he said to Thomas, "Put your finger here and see my hands. Reach out your hand and put it in my side. Do not doubt but believe." Thomas answered him, "My Lord and my God!" Jesus said to him, "Have you believed because you have seen me? Blessed are those who have not seen and yet have come to believe."

— John 20:24–29

Da pacem cordium (canon)

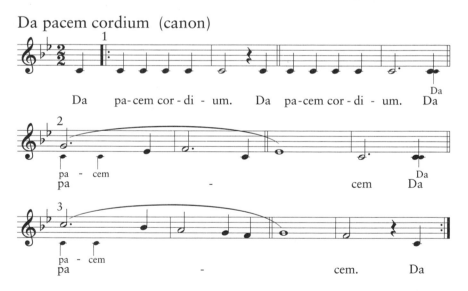

Give peace to our hearts.

Like Thomas, we were not present when Jesus rose from the dead and came back to his disciples. Like Thomas, often we would like to see and touch before believing.

Jesus does not love us any less because of our difficulty in believing. He comes again. As he did for his disciples, and especially for Thomas, he comes to us to join us in our fears and in our lack of faith.

What is striking about the risen Christ is the simplicity of his being. We could have imagined that, as the risen Lord, he would come with majesty and power. On the contrary, he is recognized by these simple words: "Peace be with you" (v. 26). The biblical word for peace, *shalom*, means much more than the absence of conflict. It is God's blessing that gives the fullness of life.

Believing in God means opening ourselves to an unexpected presence: "Do not be unbelieving but become a person of faith" (v. 27). Yes, happy are those who trust without having seen; they receive the fullness of life. As Saint Peter will write later, "Although you have not seen him, you love him; and even though you do not see him now, you believe in him and rejoice with an indescribable and glorious joy" (1 Peter 1:8).

- Jesus said to Thomas, "Do not be unbelieving but become a person of faith." What do these words mean to me?
- When I am faced with an unknown situation and could be paralyzed by it, what helps me to go beyond fear and to continue on the road of trusting?
- What does Christ's last beatitude in John's Gospel mean to me? "Blessed are those who have not seen and yet have come to believe."

Christ Jesus, when we think we are alone, you are present. If there seems to be doubt within us, that does not make you love us any the less. We would like to be daring enough to take risks on account of you, Christ. So we pay attention to your words: "Those who give their life for love will find it."

Unifying Knowledge and Love

Paul wrote, "If I have prophetic powers, and understand all mysteries and all knowledge, and if I have all faith, so as to remove mountains, but do not have love, I am nothing."

– 1 Corinthians 13:2

El alma que anda en amor

The soul filled by love neither tires others nor grows tired.

In this letter to the Corinthians, Paul resists a vision of the Christian faith that restricts itself to abstractions and theoretical understanding. With an astonishing sense of community, he refuses to accept the individualism, the divisions (see 1:11–12) and the partisan-mindedness, which an abstract Christianity had allowed to develop. The God whom Christ reveals, and who distributes the gifts of his Spirit widely, continues to carry out his plan to gather all peoples together. Spiritual gifts must necessarily be at the service of this plan (see chapters 12 and 14).

Christian faith is anchored in history, not in abstractions. It is with our bodies that we situate ourselves in reality (see chapter 5). As always for Paul, mysticism and ethics are inseparable. It is with this same body that we await the Resurrection (see chapter 15). It is true that the Resurrection has already begun, but it is also true that we await the full manifestation of the victory over death. And the consequences of this hope reach to the most tangible dimensions of life, to the body itself.

At times in this letter, we sense that the author wants to avoid being misunderstood. How could such a profoundly intelligent man be against knowledge? How can he, incomparable mystic that he was, be opposed to spiritual gifts? He certainly knew that even if the Christian faith bursts the bounds of rationality, it does not contradict reason (see 1:30). And in order to walk in faith we need to reflect (otherwise it would be a waste of time even to write to the Corinthians). But Paul joins knowledge and love. A knowledge that does not include love and guide us to it is suspect.

In chapter 13 we are able to grasp why this word "love" is so dear to Paul. The splendid hymn he writes is at the opposite extreme from an illusory sentimentality. Whoever loves with the love described in this passage will never be ensnared in a false spirituality.

- In what areas of my life am I sometimes too theoretical?
- How can the reality of love that Paul describes in chapter 13 help us to discover a way of putting our faith into practice?

Christ Jesus, even if we had faith enough to move mountains, without living charity, what would we be? You love us. Without your Holy Spirit, who lives in our hearts, what would we be? You love us. Taking everything upon yourself, you open for us a way toward trust in God, who wants neither suffering nor human distress. Spirit of the risen Christ, Spirit of compassion, Spirit of praise, your love for each one of us will never disappear.

The Light of a Face

When Jesus saw the crowds, he went up the mountain;
and after he sat down, his disciples came to him. Then he
began to speak, and taught them.

– Matthew 5:1–2a

The Beatitudes

1. Happy all, who are poor in spir-it: for the king-dom of heaven is theirs.
2. Happy all those who now are weep-ing: the joy of God will com-fort them.
3. Happy all the hum-ble, the gen-tle: for the earth one day will be theirs.
4. Happy all, who for jus-tice hun-ger: they shall re-ceive their heart's de-sire.
5. Happy all, who for-give-ness of-fer: for they shall al-so be for-given.
6. Happy all with hearts clear and sim-ple: for they shall come to see their God.
7. Happy all cre-a-tors of true peace: they shall be called chil-dren of God.
8. Happy all suff-'ring per-se-cu-tion: for the King-dom of heaven is theirs.
9. Happy all, who per-se-vere for Christ: for in God they'll be filled with joy.

This is the verse that introduces the Beatitudes. Why, before listening to this key text, and the entire Sermon on the Mount that will follow, are we asked to look at Christ? Undoubtedly because, for Matthew, the Beatitudes do not detail a philosophy, an abstract message, a teaching that could hold its own even without the presence of Jesus. The Beatitudes are only true because Jesus is there. And he is there first of all for the poor, for those who weep, those who have no room on this earth. If he is there for them, then they can be called happy.

In mentioning the crowd, the Gospel wants us to understand that what is said applies to everyone, not just to a religious elite. But by adding "his disciples came to him," Matthew completes and nuances what he has just affirmed. What is said is meant for all, but to the extent that we come close to Christ, that we set out to walk in his steps. The truth of the Beatitudes only appears for those who run the risk of living them out.

Jesus himself is the first to undertake this risk. If we open ourselves to this text, we will not find abstract truths, but the light of a face—God's own commitment and way of being present and of acting. Christ is the true poor man, totally dependent on his Father, and the one in whom the Kingdom is found. He is the one who has nowhere to lay his head and to whom the earth belongs, the being with the greatest compassion, pure of heart, peacemaker. Christ's teaching cannot be separated from his person.

- What changes in us when we understand the link between Christ's teaching and his presence among us?
- Why do you think that the word "happy" is used in the Beatitudes to describe situations where we would not spontaneously use that word?

Jesus, our hope, you come to turn us into humble people of the Gospel. Our deep desire is to understand that what is best in each of us is built up through a simple trusting, and even a child can do it.

A Pilgrimage of Trust on Earth

By faith Abraham obeyed when he was called to set out for a place that he was to receive as an inheritance; and he set out, not knowing where he was going. By faith he stayed for a time in the land he had been promised, as in a foreign land, living in tents, as did Isaac and Jacob, who were heirs with him of the same promise. For he looked forward to the city that has foundations, whose architect and builder is God. By faith he received power of procreation, even though he was too old—and Sarah herself was barren—because he considered him faithful who had promised. Therefore from one person, and this one as good as dead, descendants were born, "as many as the stars of heaven and as the innumerable grains of sand by the seashore." All of these died in faith without having received the promises, but from a distance they saw and greeted them. They confessed that they were strangers and foreigners on the earth, for people who speak in this way make it clear that they are seeking a homeland. If they had been thinking of the land that they had left behind, they would have had opportunity to return. But as it is, they desire a better country, that is, a heavenly one. Therefore, God is not ashamed to be called their God; indeed, he has prepared a city for them.

– Hebrews 11:8–16

Nada te turbe / *Nothing can trouble*

Na - da te tur - be na - da te pan - te; quien a Dios tie - ne
Noth-ing can trou-ble, noth-ing can fright-en. Those who seek God shall

na - da le fal - ta. Na - da te tur - be,
nev - er go want - ing. Noth - ing can trou - ble,

na - da te es pan - te: só - lo Dios bas - ta.
noth - ing can fright - en. God a - lone fills us.

Chapter 8 of the Letter to the Hebrews is a long meditation on faith in the life of God's people. Far from being a simple assent to intellectual truths, faith is the existential attitude of human beings who make their lives a pilgrimage. The best example of this is the figure of Abraham, who "set out, not knowing where he was going."

He was not merely drifting along, to be sure; he walked in obedience to the call from God, which separated him from his comfortable habits and opened unlimited horizons before him. The same thing was true for his wife, Sarah. Going beyond what many would consider human wisdom, she placed her confidence in the One who can even bring life out of death, with the result that, in her, the impossible became possible.

But the author of the epistle takes his analysis still further. Once the first concrete results of their trust in God were attained—a land, offspring—these women and men did not stop their journey. They continued their lives as pilgrims because they realized that beyond any particular gifts that God may grant us, it is the relationship with God that is the greatest gift of all. The author calls this "the heavenly homeland" or "the City," and for him it is the ultimate goal of the pilgrimage of faith: a total sharing of life with God that involves a shared life among all those who have set out on the road. In the final analysis, trusting in God means discovering that, beyond the signs God can and will offer us, there lies a transformation of our being itself, by which we are gradually made able to enter into all the fullness of God.

- When was I required to live my faith as a departure toward the unknown? What allowed me to set out?
- What shape does the temptation to settle down take in my life? Where can I find the energy for a new beginning?

God of all loving, you fill us with the freshness of the Gospel when a heart that trusts is at the beginning of everything.

LEARNING TO LOVE

Giving One's Life for Those One Loves

Jesus said to his disciples, "No one has greater love than this, to lay down one's life for one's friends. You are my friends if you do what I command you. I do not call you servants any longer, because the servant does not know what the master is doing; but I have called you friends, because I have made known to you everything that I have heard from my Father. You did not choose me but I chose you. And I appointed you to go and bear fruit, fruit that will last, so that the Father will give you whatever you ask him in my name. I am giving you these commands so that you may love one another."

— John 15:13–17

Grande est ta bonté / *There can be no greater love*

"No one has greater love than this, to lay down one's life for one's friends" (John 15:13). Just before his passion and resurrection, Christ summed up the meaning of his entire life in these few words: to give his life out of love.

Wherever we may be on our journey, perhaps this hope fills us too: can I make love the priority of my life, a project that matters more than anything else and that can inspire my choices and act in all the areas of my existence?

When this kind of hope is urgently felt, it can worry us. Does it have any meaning? Would it not be better to limit it? This longing comes from so deep within me that I could imagine that I am its origin and the only one responsible for it. But this would be too narrow an outlook. This longing passes through me. I am the bearer, but it comes from somewhere else, and it will only find its full meaning in the encounter with someone other than myself, someone who offers me a communion.

Christ understands this thirst within me; he knows its strength. He knows that it can disturb me, make me aware of my poverty, of my inability to give it meaning and fulfillment. But he opens a road on which it can come to full flowering, when I understand that I myself am not the source of love, just as I am not the source of joy, of peace, or of forgiveness.

- When have I discovered that I am filled with a longing that is beyond me?
- How have I found support in the searching of other persons? For whom can my own searching help to shed light on their way?

Christ Jesus, you call us to give our lives for love. And even if there is a greater or lesser degree of darkness in each of us, there is also your presence, your Holy Spirit.

Loving Life

[Peter wrote:] All of you, have unity of spirit, sympathy, love for one another, a tender heart, and a humble mind. Do not repay evil for evil or abuse for abuse; but, on the contrary, repay with a blessing. It is for this that you were called—that you might inherit a blessing. For "Those who desire life and desire to see good days, let them keep their tongues from evil and their lips from speaking deceit; let them turn away from evil and do good; let them seek peace and pursue it."

– 1 Peter 3:8–11

Qui regarde vers Dieu

Look to God and you will shine, all bitterness gone from your face.

Peter addresses those "who desire life." He agrees with the biblical tradition affirming that the goal of the commandments is to make us happy (see Deuteronomy 5:16, 29, 33, etc.). Here he gives concrete indications to seek peace, for where there is peace, life is good. Peace is fragile; it cannot be imposed. It is timid; little is required for it to flee. That is why we have to "pursue it." We need to be very attentive in order to keep walking in its steps.

First of all, we have to seek the spirit of unity. This does not necessarily mean to have the same opinions about everything. Unanimity is something deeper. It means trusting that the Holy Spirit is doing the same work in others as in me, even if at times I can only believe this and not see any concrete signs of it. Mutual love is expressed through compassion and sympathy. Those who rejoice at the happiness of others and who know how to suffer with those in trouble (see Romans 12:15) become one heart and one soul.

The spirit of humility consists in seeing in each person someone worthy of being served.

Seeking peace means not "repaying evil for evil or abuse for abuse." Christians are called to put an end to the spiral of evil that transmits wounds and humiliations from one person to another or sometimes from one generation to another. Forgiveness is the opposite of passivity. It is a form of resistance to evil, a combat to stop the spread of deadly contagion. "Blessing in order to inherit a blessing" also means, for love of life, to bandage wounds instead of opening them.

- What is necessary to make the places where we live places where life is good?
- How can we keep on loving when we are wounded by harshness?
- How can we break the cycle of humiliation by being "the last link in the chain"? How can we remove the poison and the harm from hurtful words and actions?

Christ Jesus, multitudes of children and young people have been marked for life because they were abandoned; they are like strangers on this earth. There are some who wonder: "Does my life still have any meaning?" And you assure us: each time you alleviate the suffering of an innocent person, you do it for me, Christ.

125

Making Life Beautiful Around Us

[Peter wrote:] "Above all, maintain constant love for one another, for love covers a multitude of sins."

– 1 Peter 4:8

Crucem tuam

Cru- cem tu - am a - do-ra-mus Do-mi - ne, re-sur - re-cti-o-nem

tu - am lau-da-mus Do-mi - ne. Lau-da - mus et glo-ri - fi - ca - mus.

Re-sur-rec-ti-o-nem tu-am lau-da-mus Do-mi - ne. Cru- cem tu -

We adore your cross, Lord. We praise your resurrection.

Every day it can happen that we make mistakes that may even be serious. The New Testament does not hide the fact that, already at the time of the apostles, this question arose: If the Holy Spirit has been poured out, why is it that even those who try to follow Christ sometimes do wrong?

The apostle Peter does not reply to this question directly. But he shows a way forward when people's faults and mistakes lead them to become discouraged: "Above all, maintain constant love for one another, for love covers a multitude of sins." He is inspired here by a biblical proverb: "Hatred stirs up strife, but love covers all offenses" (Proverbs 10:12). How does love "cover" wrongs, or even sins? "To cover over wrongs" is demanding. It does not mean denying them or hiding them, but struggling to take away their harmfulness, to limit their power to destroy. Love "covers" a wrong like throwing a wet towel on a fire that is beginning to burn puts it out. It is important to act quickly. Otherwise it will become difficult to extinguish the blaze before it has burnt up everything. Harsh or unthinking words, forgetfulness or negligence, failures and offenses are like sparks that can become destructive blazes. Love is able to "cover" them, to nip in the bud their formidable ability to harm.

"Covering wrongs" is the exact opposite of a passive attitude. It requires an energy that can sometimes be superhuman, the "deep love" of which Peter speaks, to neutralize wrongs that have been done. The Holy Spirit supports us in this, at times suggesting surprising ideas to make life beautiful in spite of disappointments.

- How do we react in the face of wrongs? What can we do to limit or even take away their power to harm?
- What reawakens in me a "deep love" when I am disappointed because of the blunders of others or my own mistakes?

Risen Jesus, in the plowed-up earth of our lives you come to place the trusting of faith. A small seed at first, it can become within us one of the most unmistakable Gospel realities. It sustains the inexhaustible goodness of a human heart.

Loosing the Bonds of Injustice

The Lord says:
Is not this the fast that I choose:
to loose the bonds of injustice,
to undo the thongs of the yoke,
to let the oppressed go free,
and to break every yoke?
Is it not to share your bread with the hungry,
and bring the homeless poor into your house;
when you see the naked, to cover them,
and not to hide yourself from your own kin?
Then your light shall break forth like the dawn,
and your healing shall spring up quickly;
your vindicator shall go before you,
the glory of the Lord shall be your rear guard.
Then you shall call, and the Lord will answer;
you shall cry for help, and he will say, Here I am.
If you remove the yoke from among you,
the pointing of the finger, the speaking of evil,
if you offer your food to the hungry and satisfy the
needs of the afflicted,
then your light shall rise in the darkness
and your gloom be like the noonday.
The Lord will guide you continually,
and satisfy your needs in parched places,
and make your bones strong;
and you shall be like a watered garden,
like a spring of water, whose waters never fail.

— Isaiah 58:6–11

Benedictus (canon)

Be - ne - di - ctus qui ve - nit, be - ne - di - ctus qui ve - nit, in
no - mi - ne, in no - mi - ne, in no - mi - ne Do - mi - ni.

Blessed is the one who comes in the name of the Lord.

Untying all the cords of the yoke, refusing all forms of violence... There can be a suppressed violence that takes root, very often without my knowing it, in the wounds I bear within myself. It is like a tourniquet pressing upon the heart and distorting my relationships with others. Refusing violence means placing trust at the beginning of every encounter with others.

Feeding, clothing, and giving shelter involve satisfying the needs and elementary rights of a human being. But it also means caring for, educating, listening to, giving an occupation to... in other words, recognizing and developing all that is human in the other because he or she is of my "own flesh." It also means making life possible, alleviating suffering, restoring beauty and meaning to life.

"Do not hide yourself from your own kin"; love others as you love yourself. The prophet Isaiah notes that it is this that allows my own wound to heal and for all that is in me to radiate outward. What seemed to be an ethical demand is in the first place something that allows me to become more fully human!

This then prepares a way for God's glory and the light of the Resurrection, in other words, the beauty of his love, which is an attentiveness to all that concerns human beings and their creative capacities to serve. God counts on the human heart as a way of making himself known.

- How can my life become a light and wellspring revealing the gifts and abilities of others?
- How has an encounter with someone or a commitment for others transfigured, healed, or revealed a new dimension in my life?

God of mercy, you are familiar with our longing to be a reflection of your presence and to make life beautiful for those you entrust to us.

"As I Have Loved You"

Jesus said, "Now the Son of Man has been glorified, and God has been glorified in him. If God has been glorified in him, God will also glorify him in himself and will glorify him at once. Little children, I am with you only a little longer. You will look for me; and as I said to the Jews so now I say to you, 'Where I am going, you cannot come.' I give you a new commandment, that you love one another. Just as I have loved you, you also should love one another. By this everyone will know that you are my disciples, if you have love for one another."
— John 13:31–35

Gloria, gloria (canon)

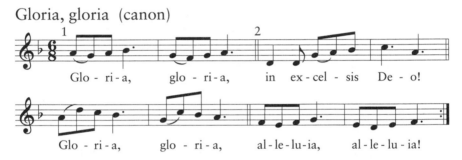

Glo - ri - a, glo - ri - a, in ex - cel - sis De - o!

Glo - ri - a, glo - ri - a, al - le - lu - ia, al - le - lu - ia!

Glory to God in the highest.

Why is it that Jesus speaks of glory at the moment he is about to be handed over to an ignominious death? (The word "glorify" is found five times in verses 31–32!) It is love that glorifies the "Son of Man." He is already "glorified" because he has loved without keeping back anything for himself. When Judas leaves to get those who are going to arrest Jesus, the die is already cast: Jesus will give his life for those he loves. The glory of love will shine forever on the cross. "God will glorify him in himself and will glorify him at once." That means: God will raise up Jesus so that henceforth he can love always and everywhere, giving himself as the life of the world with no limits in time and space.

Jesus knows that, in their sadness or their confusion, the disciples will look for him. So he tells them where they can find him. Not in a place far away and inaccessible, but in the love they will have for one another. Christ leaves with them, as a testament, the commandment to love one another. This is a "new commandment" because Christ does more than just give an order or an example. As the inheritance he leaves them, he places his love in the hearts of his followers. In the Gospel according to Saint John, the new commandment fills the precise place where someone familiar with the other gospels would expect to find the Eucharist. Christ gives us the ability to love by giving himself. God does not merely express his will; he works in us what he expects of us.

And not only do believers encounter Christ in their mutual love, but this love is, likewise, the only reality that makes the content of their faith credible and accessible to others (see v. 35).

- Where can I find Christ?
- How can we make faith credible to those around us?

Jesus, joy of our hearts, when the desire to fulfill what you expect of us comes welling up inside us, we understand that you invite us to love, just as you love us.

"That They May All Be One"

Jesus prayed, "I ask not only on behalf of these here present, but also on behalf of those who will believe in me through their word, that they may all be one. As you, Father, are in me and I am in you, may they also be in us, so that the world may believe that you have sent me."

– John 17:20–21

Rendez grâce au Seigneur / O give thanks

Al - lé - lu - ia, al - lé - lu - ia, al - lé - lu - ia.

1. Ren - dez grâ - ce au Sei - gneur, car il est bon,
1. O give thanks for the good - ness of the Lord,

é - ter - nel est son a - mour al - lé - lu - ia!
for God's love will nev - er end, al - le - lu - ia!

2. Ren - dez grâ - ce à Jé - sus Res - sus - ci - té,
2. O give thanks for the Ris - en Christ our Lord,

é - ter - nel est son a - mour, al - lé - lu - ia!
for God's love will nev - er end, al - le - lu - ia!

3. Ren - dez grâ - ce à l'Es - prit Cré - a - teur,
3. O give thanks for the Spir - it of life,

é - ter - nel est son a - mour, al - lé - lu - ia!
for God's love will nev - er end, al - le - lu - ia!

Jesus makes the growth of faith depend upon the unity of the disciples among themselves, of which the foundation and model are found in his communion with the Father.

This unity of Christ's friends, essential so "that the world may believe," is combined with their being sent out on the mission that Jesus entrusts to them: "Go into all the world and proclaim the good news to the whole creation" (Mark 16:15).

Christians are invited to live this twofold fidelity, to being sent out and to unity, not as two poles that are antagonistic but as two sides of the same coin. Unity precedes and gives substance to their witness. At the same time, this unity is called to grow wider, to become a lived and proclaimed reality within the context of a Church that is expanding geographically, that embraces the diversity of cultures and of peoples as it makes its way through history, lasting from one generation to another, one age to the next.

Living out our faith, trusting in God, therefore, commits us to seeking communion first of all. Mutual love becomes the primary criterion that guides our search for truth, for service, or our prayer.

People who commit themselves to communion are doing what is essential so that the world may believe, so that the wellsprings of trust may be made accessible and so that others may discover them. "The reality is the Body of Christ" (Colossians 2:17).

This unity is not an inaccessible ideal, which would lead only to discouragement. It already exists in the communion of the Father, Son, and Holy Spirit. That is the source of our vocation and our incentive to go forward. Human beings are called to reproduce the likeness of the God who is Trinity by being different persons within the unity of the same communion.

- In what situations is the responsibility for unity entrusted to me?
- How can we live this unity, this "remaining together," which is necessary in sharing our faith with others, in a context where we are scattered or have little time and energy?
- How is my personal witness linked to a commitment in the life of a local community?

Living God, we praise you for the multitudes of women, men, young people, and children who, across the earth, are striving to be witnesses to peace, trust, and reconciliation. The steps of the holy witnesses of all the ages, from the apostles and the Virgin Mary down to those of today, enable us day after day to dispose ourselves inwardly to place our trust in the Mystery of the Faith.

You Are God's Joy

At that same hour Jesus rejoiced in the Holy Spirit and said, "I thank you, Father, Lord of heaven and earth, because you have hidden these things from the wise and the intelligent and have revealed them to infants; yes, Father, for such was your gracious will. All things have been handed over to me by my Father; and no one knows who the Son is except the Father, or who the Father is except the Son and anyone to whom the Son chooses to reveal him."

– Luke 10:21–22

Jubilate cœli (canon) / *Heavens, sing with gladness*

Joy is often perceived as the end result of our own efforts, for instance, as the satisfaction found in having done something well, often as a fleeting instant in what is otherwise a life full of worries. In scripture, however, joy is present at every new beginning: as the angels sing for the newborn Christ-child on that first Christmas eve, heavy with threats of violence; with the disciples at Easter even before they have fully grasped what is happening; proclaimed at Pentecost when the comforting Spirit opens the doors and enables the marvels of God to be expressed in every tongue.

Joy is present, too, at the start of every encounter. This jubilation of Jesus in the Gospel is an invitation to discover it for ourselves. Other people are a source of joy not because of the satisfaction they can bring me, but because each one is loved by God in a unique manner and has been entrusted to me. You are God's joy, and the Lord wishes that you be my joy, too. God wishes that the Holy Spirit may enlighten my eyes, ready as I so often am to judge others. He wants my heart to be made more encompassing, and an expectant hope to be awoken in me.

I am not responsible for creating my own joy (otherwise, my whole life would be torn between the search for satisfaction and the threat of discouragement), but I am responsible for longing for it continually. I am responsible for entrusting to God all the obstacles I meet and for allowing him to change my heart of stone into a heart capable of love. Could this be the road the starets Saint Seraphim of Sarov found, which led him to greet each one of his visitors with the words, "My joy!"?

- What helps me to see "my joy" in each person I meet?
- What "little ones" are sources of gratefulness in my life?

Christ, for each person you desire joy, a happiness straight from the Gospel. And the peace of our heart can make life beautiful for those around us.

"You Are the Light of the World"

Jesus said to his disciples, "You are the salt of the earth; but if salt has lost its taste, how can its saltiness be restored? It is no longer good for anything, but is thrown out and trampled under foot. You are the light of the world. A city built on a hill cannot be hid. No one after lighting a lamp puts it under the bushel basket, but on the lampstand, and it gives light to all in the house. In the same way, let your light shine before others, so that they may see your good works and give glory to your Father in heaven."

– Matthew 5:13–16

Gloria ... et in terra pax (canon)

Glo- ri - a,   glo - ri - a   in ex - cel - sis De - o,

glo - ri - a,   glo - ri - a,   al - le - lu - ia!

Et in ter - ra pax ho - mi - ni - bus

bo - næ vo - lun - ta - tis.

Glory to God in the highest and on earth peace to people of good will.

Speaking to a crowd that was surely very diverse, Jesus expressed what he saw in them. "You are the salt of the earth... the light of the world." We can imagine how surprised his hearers must have been! He wasn't talking about the future, but about the present. He didn't say, "One day you will be... if...," but "You *are...*" Christ sees the hidden depths of those who listen to him, their deepest identities, and he wants to reveal them. When we read these words, Christ makes us, too, realize what we are, what our eyes do not yet see.

Salt of the earth. Like food, Jesus seems to say, human life needs to be seasoned. How can we live if life seems tasteless? By their search for the living God and for his kingdom, those who listen to Christ give this taste to all those whom they meet. More than by this or that personal quality, they awaken others to a taste for life by their longing for God.

Light of the world. The two following images, that of a city on a hilltop and a lamp in a house, express the fact that it is unthinkable to wish to hide what already exists and gives light. What we have to do, says Jesus, is not so much to display the gift God has already given us, but simply not to hide it. We are simply asked to let the light God has placed in us shine out. Through "your good works," in other words our concern for those who are nearby, another presence makes itself felt, close to us.

- Among people I know, who is like "the salt of the earth" or "the light of the world"? What strikes me about them?
- How do the words of Christ illuminate my life and familiar situations? How can I realize that Christ speaks these words— "you are the salt of the earth and the light of the world"—to me, and dare to take them seriously?

Jesus, peace of our hearts, where the trusting of faith has been shaken, make us bearers of your Gospel, and keep us close to those who are beset by doubts.

Loving with Compassion

Jesus said, "If you do good to those who do good to you, what credit is that to you? For even sinners do the same. If you lend to those from whom you hope to receive, what credit is that to you? Even sinners lend to sinners, to receive as much again. But love your enemies, do good, and lend, expecting nothing in return. Your reward will be great, and you will be children of the Most High; for he is kind to the ungrateful and the wicked.

"Be merciful, just as your Father is merciful. Do not judge, and you will not be judged; do not condemn, and you will not be condemned. Forgive, and you will be forgiven; give, and it will be given to you. A good measure, pressed down, shaken together, running over, will be put into your lap; for the measure you give will be the measure you get back."

– Luke 6:33–38

I am sure I shall see

I am sure I shall see the good-ness of the Lord in the land of the liv-ing. Yes, I shall see the good-ness of our God; hold firm, trust in the Lord. I am

How can we understand the words of Jesus: "Do not judge; do not condemn"? It has sometimes been thought that they refer to the excessive harshness of some judgments. But if that were the idea, why could Jesus not have said, "Judge with moderation; do not condemn harshly"? What did he mean, then? The words that follow can help us go in the right direction. Jesus adds, "You will not be judged; you will not be condemned." He does not only invite us not to judge others. His words also free us from the worry of being judged ourselves, of the judgment we might deserve. They take us out of the world of rights and judgments.

We can move away from "justice" in two different directions. On the one hand there is injustice. But on the other hand, there is that new form of existence the Gospel calls the Kingdom of God. The welcome offered to the prodigal son and the salary the workers of the eleventh hour receive (see Luke 15:11–32 and Matthew 22:1–16) are not, strictly speaking, "just." But the measure of God's Kingdom, compassion, is of another order. It is "a good measure, pressed down, shaken together, running over" (v. 38).

When we try to fix a situation by criticisms and demands, in the best case we obtain what we consider fair and just. But what if God wanted to give us more, to open before us an unexpected horizon? The Kingdom of God is that surprise. One day, Jesus said to those who were working hard to make things better by means of judgments and condemnations, "You do not go into the kingdom of heaven yourselves, and when others are going in, you stop them" (Matthew 23:13). Not judging means keeping our eyes open to see the miracle of God and welcoming it in other people and in our own lives.

- What does "loving with compassion" mean for me?
- In what situations do criticisms and demands shut doors and keep us from discovering what God wants to give us?

Holy Spirit, mystery of a presence, you penetrate the depths of our being, and there you discern a longing. You know what our intention is—to communicate your compassion through an infinite goodness of heart.

A Life Given for Love

*Jesus said, "Those who want to save their life will lose it,
and those who lose their life for my sake will save it."*
— Luke 9:24

Laudate Dominum / *Sing, praise and bless the Lord*

Lau - da - te   Do - mi - num,   lau - da - te
Sing,   praise   and   bless the Lord.   Sing,   praise   and

Do - mi - num,   om - nes   gen - tes,
bless   the   Lord.   Peo - ples!   Na - tions!

1. Al - le - lu - ia!   2. Al - le - lu - ia!
Al - le - lu - ia!   Al - le - lu - ia!

Jesus came so that people might have "life to the full"; he came to save "those who were lost." He did not wish to repress human life, therefore, but to liberate it from all that could hamper it.

People who think only about saving themselves live under the threat of failure. Making their fears the motivation of their acts, they live on the defensive, attempting to protect themselves, refusing to look for something new. In the end, other people become rivals or threats.

Whoever gives their life is freed from constantly having to calculate: "What will I get out of it? What will I lose?" If they consent to "lose," in their own eyes as well as in the eyes of others, that is because the free gift of themselves is already vital for them and is more meaningful than anything else. Rather than seeking to convince others, to control or to seduce, they can serve others, care for them, support them. In this way they create trust. Their freedom blossoms in a communion without limits; their existence can open to eternal life.

There is a sequence in giving. If I am alive, if I am able to love life, that is because others have loved me and looked forward to welcoming me. And if I want others to have a beautiful life, it is because I know that life is worth living. Since I have received my life from another, I can give it in my turn.

Jesus is the perfect witness to the truth that life takes on its full meaning when it is given. Because, as Son of God, he lived to the very end a life rooted in the Father's love, he was able to give his own life, his body and his blood, out of love for human beings. In his eyes, we matter more than his own existence. His gift becomes for us a source that enables us to give ourselves. By relying on him, we have, beyond our failings and our fears, the assurance that we, too, can live lives of love.

- How can I invite others to marvel at what I love most in life?
- What reminds me of the value that God places on human beings, on creation, and on life?

Jesus, our joy, by remaining in your presence, we realize that the Gospel calls us to give our lives. Even if we forget you, your love remains, and you send your Holy Spirit upon us.